1

The Successful Bloggers Guide

Including The Blog Advertising Manual

by Sleepy Dragon Marketing

Table of Contents

3

Understanding Blogging

What Blogging Is All About

Defining Blogging

A blog is a type of website or part of a website. It gets its name from the term "web log" which originally referred to an online log of partner websites, personal updates and newsworthy items. Blogs are usually maintained by an individual with regular entries of commentary, descriptions of events, or other material such as graphics or video. Entries are commonly displayed in reverse-chronological order. "Blog" can also be used as a verb, meaning to maintain or add content to a blog.

Most blogs are interactive, allowing visitors to leave comments and even message each other via widgets on the blogs and it is this interactivity that distinguishes them from other static websites.

Many blogs provide commentary or news on a particular subject; others function as more personal online diaries. A typical blog combines text, images, and links to other blogs, Web pages, and other media related to its topic. The ability of readers to leave comments in an interactive format is an important part of many blogs. Most blogs are primarily textual; some focus on art, photographs, videos, music, and audio (podcasting). Micro-blogging is another type of blogging, featuring very short posts.

Before blogging became popular, digital communities took many forms, including Usenet, commercial online services such as GEnie, BiX and the early CompuServe, e-mail lists and Bulletin Board Systems (BBS). In the 1990s, Internet forum software created running conversations with "threads." Threads are topical connections between messages on a bulletin board websites. They are so named because they have an initial topic and then a string of follow-up comments in some type of chronological order. A forum could have many sub-forums with many topics and many strings of conversations and replies.

The modern blog evolved from the online diary, where people would keep a running account of their personal lives. Most such writers called themselves diarists, journalists, or "journalers." Justin Hall, who began personal blogging in 1994 while a student at Swarthmore College, is generally recognized as one of the earliest bloggers, as is Jerry Pournelle. Dave Winer's Scripting News is also credited with being one of the oldest and longest running weblogs. Another early blog was Wearable Wireless Webcam, an online shared diary of a person's personal life combining text, video and pictures transmitted live from a wearable computer and EyeTap device to a web site in 1994. This practice of semi-automated blogging with live video together with text was referred to as sousveillance, and such journals were also used as evidence in legal matters.

Early blogs were simply manually updated components of common Web sites. However, the evolution of tools to facilitate the production and maintenance of Web articles posted in reverse chronological order made the publishing process feasible to a much larger, less technical, population. Ultimately, this resulted in the distinct class of online publishing that produces blogs we recognize today. For instance, the use of some sort of browser-based software is now a typical aspect of blogging. Blogs can be hosted by dedicated blog hosting services, or they can be run using blog software, or on regular web hosting services.

Characteristics of Blogs

While not every blog is alike, most share a few common threads that help distinguish them from other Websites on the Internet. Some of the basic features found in many blogs include:

- **Short posts** – Blogs are not generally designed to accommodate long posts. In most cases, blog entries run between 200 and 1,000 words. This makes them fairly easy to update and provides readers with information in a quick fashion.
- **Frequent updates** – Well-run blogs tend to contain a lot of content (articles or posts). These posts are updated regularly to give visitors reasons to keep coming back for more.
- **Conversational style** – While some blogs are written in a more formal, newsy manner, this format is ideal for the conversational style, as well. In branding, the conversational style can greatly help build a feeling of direct communication with readers (customers), which can help build a sense of loyalty and a connection.
- **Commenting ability** – Not every blog enables readers to post comments and ask questions of writers, but many do. For branding efforts, this can prove quite valuable. Branding involves the act of building on all the key ingredients in a successful business and then putting them in a package that customers can readily identify. Branding builds recognition for a product. So, when comments are enabled, readers and the branding company can open up two-way dialogue, which can prove extremely useful for developing rapport.

Additional Features of Blogs

Blogs can vary greatly in specific style and inclusion of special features. They may, for example, exist on their own, separate from a corporate Website. They may also be found attached to or even built within a corporate site. Other features that can help make them more appealing for readers and useful for branding efforts include:

- **Photo images** – Full color images are often used to support individual posts. These can be especially helpful when working on a branding effort. When the products and/or services in question are put out on the Internet in full color, recognition for the brand can grow.

- **Videos** – It is not at all uncommon for videos to also be used within the blog format. In branding, videos may be used to show off a product or service or even demonstrate how it is used.

- **Forums** – This takes standard blog comments sections to the next level. Rather than limiting communications to small fields, an auxiliary forum can promote an even more open exchange of information.

- **Auxiliary newsletters** – Some blogs are supported by the creation of auxiliary newsletters that are e-mailed directly to visitors who subscribe. The inclusion of a newsletter signup on a blog is an excellent way for a company to gain its own preauthorized e-mailing list. It is also excellent for backing up branding efforts with one more communications tool that is affordable.

There is no set-in-stone format for what a blog should be or must be. That's part of the beauty of this type of vehicle. Companies, organizations or individuals who are working on branding efforts are perfectly free to customize their creation to fit their own specific strengths and needs. This makes the tool extremely flexible and appropriate for just about any type of branding effort.

Blogging Today

Blogging is more popular than ever these days and it's one of the most profitable advertising markets next to social networking websites. Where only a few blogs existed on the Internet in the 1990s, the blogosphere is now filled with thousands of sites. Blogs today are written for a wide variety of reasons. Some bloggers write simply to connect with their own friends and family, others share political views or discuss hobbies, still others use this unique tool to promote their brand and foster a connection with readers or customers.

Blogs have the distinct benefit of being absolutely loved by search engine bots and offering easy link-back opportunities in the form of comment posts. Blogs are devilishly easy to update and customize and since they require very little maintenance, they can be very inexpensive. Some very popular and very profitable websites are created only with blog software. The beauty of the software is that you can customize it to the point where it doesn't look like "just a blog." Blogs are one of the most powerful tools an Internet marketer has today.

One of the primary ways of profiting from blogs is through ad programs like Google's AdSense. This only *makes* sense if you have a lot of traffic, so getting clicks is the absolute key. Another way to make even more money is to charge for direct advertising space. This bypasses Google's commission, although it does make it a bit harder to get advertisers in the first place.

Affiliate linking is also a great way of bringing in income. Instead of directly using your blog for advertising revenue you provide affiliate advertisement in the form of blog posts; you use a special link with a reference number that will give you a percentage of the profit if the person who used the link buys the product (You set these up with your affiliate websites). Of course, how much money you'll ultimately make on any advertising paradigm depends on a number of factors.

You have to consider how popular your blog is, how many link backs you have and how many daily visitors you get. Your popularity, daily visitors and link backs depend ultimately on the overall value of your blog, which is controlled by the quality relevancy of your blog posts. So, as you can see, writing a good and effective blog goes hand-in-hand with using your blog to make money. A crummy, ill-formatted blog will not get you any daily visitors and with no daily visitors, you're useless to any advertisers or affiliates.

When a blog is used to its full advantage it will not only enable you to reach out to clients and potential clients, but it will give them the ability to reach out to you as well. This two-way communication can serve as a powerful means for developing rapport, trust and repeat business.

In this book, we'll not only go over the various ways you can create income from blogs, but we'll talk about how to make high-quality, easily manageable blogs that attract visitors as well.

Blogging for Business

How Blogging Benefits Your Business

Blog Versatility

Blogs are extremely flexible and have the potential to be so effective that there really isn't a business out there that cannot benefit from the use of this vehicle. In fact, for some people, blogging is actually their paying business. This tool can add onto branding efforts no matter the product, service or idea that is in the spotlight. The blog itself can even be the "brand" in question.

Some examples that show just how versatile blogging can be in building a brand and cultivating business interests include:

Product blogs – Blogs that are designed to promote a specific company and its products might contain news about upcoming releases, how present products are used and other related tidbits of information.

Service blogs – Companies that sell services rather than specific products often use blogs to share information about their industry, to share tips on how to tell when a service call is needed and so on.

Professional blogs – Doctors, lawyers, accountants and other professionals use blogs to get their names out on the Internet and to share vital information with readers. A doctor, for example, might write posts about maintaining health, how to tell if someone is sick and what to expect from certain treatments. This type of blog builds on the professional's own brand.

Government blogs – Many governmental agencies on the city, county, state and federal levels now use blogs to impart important information to citizens. These blogs can range from highly newsy and formal in style to very conversational. The idea is to create an outlet to quickly and effectively share news and information with residents.

Artistic blogs – Published authors, journalists, artists, musicians and others in the creative fields use blogs to boost their own brand recognition. They often use these vehicles to update fans on their current projects, to share personal news and more.

Niche blogs – In some cases, the brand is the blog itself. Some entrepreneurs create blogs geared to a specific topic and build themselves up as authorities on the said topic. To generate income, they sell advertising on their blogs or act as affiliate marketers for products related to the niche. The better the branding efforts here, the more likely it is the blog will be able to establish itself as a reliable authority on the subject matter. This, in turn, can build the brand and traffic on the site at the same time. When these two things happen, advertising or affiliate revenues can go up thanks to the exposure received.

Organizational blogs – Many nonprofit organizations now use blogs to connect with their supporters. These blogs might contain information about fundraising efforts, public appearances, current public service campaigns and more. Blogs have proven very effective for helping build the brand recognition of different nonprofit organizations while also assisting them in gaining support and even reaching out to clients they service.

The beauty of blogs is that they can be used in a variety of ways to reach out to readers and build and maintain a following. The exposure gained through this format can prove to be a very powerful force in building a brand and the business behind it.

How Blogging Helps Your Business

Do not underestimate the power a blog can have for building the recognition of a particular brand. When a blog becomes a force on the Internet within its own specific niche, traffic numbers can go through the ceiling. Keep in mind that traffic on a Website is similar to customers walking in through a front door – some will purchase products and services. The more traffic obtained, the more likely it is success will follow.

When a blog is successful, ranks high with the search engines and garners a lot of traffic, it can pay off by:

Building brand name recognition – The more visitors a blog pulls in, the more people around the globe will hear about a particular brand. When this exposure is coupled with a solid product, service or company and other branding efforts, people will become more familiar with the brand and more comfortable with it.

Creating a buzz for a brand or product – The exposure gained from blogging can get people talking about a specific brand. This builds word-of-mouth advertising and can greatly impact the number of customers a company receives.

Increasing direct sales – When blogging efforts pique client interest, the real results can show up in the bottom line. The more a brand is understood and talked about, the more likely it is people will trust the brand's products enough to purchase whatever is being sold. Whether your company sells cereal, offers a service or simply writes a blog as an authority on a specific topic and generates revenue from advertising on the blog, exposure can result in bottom line growth.

The Many Advantages of Blogging

Whether it is used on its own or, more appropriately, as part of a multipronged branding campaign, blogging does have its share of advantages. Blogs tend to be:

Highly affordable – Launching a blog is something that can literally be done on a shoestring budget. It costs next to nothing to establish an effective blog. While it is certainly feasible to put a sizeable investment into the effort by hiring pros for design and writing, these expenses are not necessarily required. Pros can make blogs and the sites they are built on look and present better, but costs can be kept down through a do-it-yourself job when necessary.

Popular – The short, to-the-point format of most blogs makes them highly popular with readers all over the globe. The credibility of some blogs as authorities on their specific topics is helping this format gain greatly in popularity. Consider how many blogs are now spotlighted in the news and the growth in popularity will become evident.

Very flexible – While companies and organizations might have (and probably should have) style guidelines for their blogs, the format remains highly flexible. This is a creative outlet for reaching out, creating brand recognition and communicating with readers.

Easy to update – The relatively loose style makes it fairly easy to keep a blog updated. It is not necessary to have highly polished, multipage posts put online every day to reap the rewards of blogging. Even a short post of 200 or 300 words can be useful for updating a blog and ensuring its content is fresh. While quality pieces are essential, they do not have to take up a tremendous amount of time to produce.

Fun – Maintaining a blog and learning to use the tool to capture an audience is actually a fun undertaking. This is one of the most enjoyable ways to reach out and connect personally with clients and potential clients.

Blogging is an effective, low-cost way to gain attention for a particular brand. The audience on the Internet is potentially endless as more people get online and it stretches well across international boundaries. This means companies can reach out and literally grow their businesses on a global level using this high-tech, low-dollar tool.

The versatility of blogs makes them perfect for any branding campaign. From international corporations, to individuals working on at-home businesses, blogs are fast becoming a highly prized vehicle for communicating brand messages and building relationships with clients.

The First Step

Setting Up Your Blog

Blog Platforms

Setting up your blog will require a little research and review; you'll need to consider the factors of cost, the time and skills you currently have, and your readiness to learn some new software. Almost all blog software is very easy to use and offers a variety of plug-ins and other resources to make yours unique. You don't necessarily need to hire a professional or specialist to start publishing; most blogs can be setup with a few hours, and you can learn how to use them as you go.

Blogging Programs

There are a number of different programs available on the Internet that enable people to easily and automatically set up their own blogs. These programs are typically offered for free or at a low-cost charge. The technical savvy behind these programs is so high, in fact, that many professional programmers use them instead of reinventing the wheel when a customer wants a blog built into a company Web site.

Some of the more common blogging programs available include:

- **Blogger** – Located online at www.blogger.com, this is Google's own vehicle for blogging. This program is offered free of charge and is even equipped to easily accept paid ads from Google. It provides bloggers the ability to design their own blogs and supports a number of add-ins like photos and videos. Because of its flexibility, it is often selected by professionals to serve as the "back end" program for a custom designed Website that has a built-in blog.

- **WordPress** – Located online at www.wordpress.org, this is an independent blogging program offered free of charge. It also offers a lot of bells and whistles that other programs may not and does adapt to enable users to fully customize their blog appearance. Like Blogger, WordPress works extremely well as a back end program included in the makeup of a professional site. The flexibility of this particular program has made it very popular with pros. This is the blogging tool used by such companies as Yahoo! and The New York Times.

- **Others** – There are many other blogging programs available on their own, or offered directly by Web hosting companies. Most Web hosting companies, in fact, offer the ability to "plug in" a blog during the design phase of a personal or business Website. Some companies make sure their Website design programs specifically support Blogger or WordPress. Others provide their users with different programs, which offer similar functions.

Determining Which Blog Platform to Use

You'll find a number of free and low-cost fee-based blog platforms available, and most of them use a simple text editor box for publishing. The cost differences vary depending on the type of blog you are running; if you are going to host the blog on your own domain, you will need to manage hosting fees. Blogs run within the blog's domain are usually free, but you will not have a simple address to work with. If you want a unique URL, it's better to consider the different packages, even if you're starting out with the very basic.

Most basic packages allow you to add your own design elements and start making money with advertisements immediately. Most free hosts will not allow advertising, which limits your ability to start generating a separate stream of income from ad-clicks and sales. If you're just starting out, it's best to pick the basic version so you can at least start driving traffic to advertisements.

Next, you'll need to consider how much you know about blog design. If you're already proficient with web design and templates, this will be fairly easy, but if you do not know where to start there are plenty of blog templates available. Blog templates can help you construct your basic site, and then change it later when you need to. These can be easily replaced with a more comprehensive design, but most blog platforms provide a variety of options, colors, and basic attributes to make your blog stand out.

Blog platforms such as WordPress can be very helpful in getting you setup with a professional look, especially if you have limited design skills and are not working with a web or graphic designer immediately. Blogger also offers customizable options, and you'll find a range of colors and styles to choose from. Moveable type is somewhat limited, but you can still find a basic, well-organized template.

Blog Set Up Basics

Even though each blog platform has different elements and plug-ins available, you'll need to come up with some ideas of your basic blog set up and structure. This is comprised of the types and categories of information you intend to share with the audience. For example, you will need to create content for your:

- Profile page/About Us section

- A contact page
- Resources
- Blog categories for each type of news
- Deciding whether to accept comments
- Basic marketing elements such as a blogroll or link exchange
- Space for advertising
- Feeds
- Ad Sense sections
- Logos
- Blog archives
- Page headers

After identifying the basic elements of your blog, it's time to choose the actual platform you will be using. It's not a good idea to switch platforms at a later date, since you'll probably end up reformatting and editing every piece of content. Choosing the right fit from the start is the best way to keep things moving along smooth and simply.

How to Use Blogger

Blogger is a widely-used blogging platform because of its ease of use and simple templates. You'll find a number of startup blogs that use blogger to publish online, and anything with a '.blogspot.com' extension indicates that it is a Blogger blog. Blogger is free to use, and only requires a username and password for setup and access.

You won't need to install any special software to get started, this blog platform uses a simple WYSIWIG editor. Once you've registered for your free account, you can choose a template and just start copying and pasting content into the publishing toolbar. If you need to add images, just use the upload image tool and paste it right in. Blogger is one of the most user-friendly blogging platforms available and very useful for beginners. You'll find enough fonts and color options to make your blog stand out from other sites, and can upgrade to your own domain very easily.

Step-by-Step Guide to Creating a Blogger Post

You can start blogging with a Blogger blog in just a few minutes; after registration and choosing a template, you can start posting immediately.

- **Step 1: Registration**

  The first step is to register with your name and e-mail address; using your Gmail account will help make this step much easier.

- **Step 2: Enter your basic information**

  This is where you will enter your e-mail address, a nickname, and set your password. You will also be asked to agree to the terms of service.

- **Step 3: Naming the blog**

  This is where you will enter the blog's title, and you can see how it appears as an extension of the .blogspot.com URL. If your first choice is taken, Blogger will make some recommendations or ask you to try something else.

- **Step 4: Choosing a template**

  This is where you'll choose from the gallery of templates; look for something that complements your brand, or start with a basic black and white design. Remember that you can always change this later.

- **Step 5: Start publishing**

  You can start posting right away, and a good place to start is your contact information. Make sure to include all relevant contact information, website URL's, and other information that you think your readers will find valuable.

- **Step 6: Publish with one click!**

  After entering your title, you will be all set to publish and can see the results immediately.

Using WordPress

WordPress is quickly becoming a leader of blog platforms, and offers a more professional look and easier navigation than blogger. WordPress is also compatible with a variety of content management systems, so if you are looking for something that may integrate with your commercial website at a later date, WordPress will be your best choice out of the three.

WordPress makes it easy to upload images, create categories, and works well in different browsers. It may also have some SEO benefits since each posting can be easily tagged and therefore searched by the search engines.

From a blog setup point of view, WordPress also takes just minutes to set up. You'll want to start at the WordPress homepage and can download and install the WordPress software for free. WordPress makes it very easy to add text, images, and even movie files so if you're looking for something that can offers media-rich content, this will be your best choice.

You can choose a free blog on the WordPress domain at wordpress.com, or set up a blog on your own web host. WordPress offers a variety of quality hosting programs and services right on the site; take some time to review costs and benefits of DreamHost, HostICan, Laughing Squid, and BlueHost to find out what works best for you. Most of them offer a high amount of disk storage space, competitive monthly transfer rates, and unlimited domains under one account.

Step-by-Step Guide to Creating a WordPress Post

You'll need to start by downloading and installing the WordPress software program, and then get started with the signup process.

- **Step 1: Registration**
  You'll start by entering a username, password, and an e-mail address. After accepting the terms of service, you'll be asked to name and describe your blog.
- **Step 2: Choosing a blog name**
  This is where you can choose the title and header of your blog, along with a brief 2-3 line description. Keep in mind that this will be added to the WordPress database immediately, and will be viewable to the audience whether or not you publish content right away.
- **Step 3: Verify your authentication code**
  WordPress will send you an e-mail to verify your identity and introduce you to your new blog.
- **Step 4: Choose a template**

You can choose from over ten attractive WordPress themes and templates, and can switch these out whenever you choose. WordPress also allows you to upload logos or your own design if you choose.

- **Step 5: Navigating the dashboard**
  After confirming your site, you will have a chance to enter through the dashboard. Just login with your username and password.

- **Step 6: Review the Manage, Posts, and Categories links**
  The 'Write' tab is located I the top-left hand corner. This is where you'll be able to post content directly into the editor, and the easiest way to do this is to copy and paste directly from your favorite word processing program, or enter the information as you go along.

- **Step 7: Adding images**
  WordPress allows you upload image files by clicking on the 'upload' bottom at the bottom of the page, and attaching the image. After you have uploaded it, you will need to select it for appropriate placement.

- **Step 8: Save and Publish**
  It's important to always save your work as WordPress does not do this automatically. When you save a draft it will be available for viewing in the 'Manage' tab and you can go in and edit for publishing later. Pushing 'Publish' will send the information immediately to your blog.

WordPress offers a variety of plug-ins and other tools as you get more comfortable with the overall format and design. It's a good idea to spend a few hours navigating through your options for setup and design, and there are also many WordPress forums and resource sites available when you're ready to upgrade. WordPress offers great value for businesses of all sizes, and can be customized very easily.

Other Factors to Consider

Another important consideration after setting up your blog is the amount and frequency of your postings. It may be helpful to create a schedule for posting, and almost all blog platforms allow you set a time and date stamp so you can control when things appear on your blog. This can be helpful when you want to pull together a batch of posts and release them one by one. Doing this will make sure that your blog is continuously updated, and you can choose to do this once per week, once per day, or even every hour if you want to!

This strategy will help you to plan ahead and provide quality content on a regular basis. Remember that many readers simply subscribe to your blog through the RSS reader, and having something fresh and new available on a regular basis will help them stay 'in touch.' You'll also be able to earn recognition from search engines, since the crawlers are constantly looking for websites that are constantly updated.

Organization

Understanding how each element of your blog comes together is essential for the long-term success for your business blog. After you've gained some experience with using the platform you've chosen, it's a good idea to take a close look at each area and learn what can, and perhaps cannot be, optimized to suit you best. Besides the visitor traffic counts, the overall structure and pieces of your blog can help to increase exposure.

Do keep in mind that every area of the blog can help your site become more search engine-friendly. Not only does this reduce overall marketing costs when you are trying to obtain search engine rankings, but you'll also start to see more 'organic' traffic simply by tweaking a few areas.

Everything from the blog layout, the template you choose, and the fonts and colors you use will have an impact on your final blog. You'll want to choose wisely when it comes to each area, especially paying attention to color schemes and other themes that may help with branding purposes.

Blog Layout and Composition

The layout is a part of your blog design, and your goal is to create something that will leave a lasting impression. More and more blog networks are creating 'generic' blogs that have very little creativity and are focused more on the new content instead. Even though the content of your blog is the critical element, what the visitor sees and feels as they explore your blog is just as important.

If you choose a simple layout and design, just makes sure to navigate it yourself and see what your focal point is. Are you focusing too much on the sidebars? Is the header distracting? Can you easily read the content, or do you have to squint to make sense of the font and style? All of these elements will be unique to your blog, and since it may be an extension of your company and brand, it's vital that you use something that will make a lasting impression.

The blog layout consists of:
- Fonts
- Color themes
- Line spacing
- Header styles
- Image boxes
- Advertising space
- Columns (one-, two-, or three-columns)

Color Themes and Palettes

The first step in constructing an appropriate layout involves the color theme. You want to use colors that either match or complement your main website, or even just go along with your printed materials. Remember the value in branding, especially if you have traditionally been an offline company and are now moving things ahead on the web.

Color psychology can have a positive or negative effect on every single visitor that reaches your site, and you can make the most of your branding strategy by using special colors that evoke specific feelings. The following colors are generally associated with different emotions, feelings, and reactions in both positive and negative ways:

- **Red:**
excitement, warmth, energy, and stimulating in the positive, but aggression and excessive visual impact in the negative. Red is a strong and powerful color, and can be used properly in subtle ways. It demands attraction and recognition, but can also be perceived as overly aggressive.

- **Blue:**
intelligent, cool, efficient, and trustworthy in the positive, but unfriendly and aloof in the negative. Blue is essentially soothing, and the different hues can create a peaceful and

serene feeling. However, it can also be perceived as cold and unemotional so you will need to pick the right tone to deliver the appropriate message.

- **Yellow:**

confident, creative, strong, and friendly in the positive; depressing, irrational, and even fearful in the negative. Yellow is a very stimulating and energizing color, but overusing it or using the wrong tone can work against you.

- **Green:**

balance, rest, peace, environmentally friendly in the positive, but bored, bland, and stagnant in the negative. Green can be used in very positive ways for a refreshing and energizing color palette, but too many dark tones can be perceived negatively.

- **Orange:**

warmth, security, fun, and abundance in the positive, but frivolity and disorder in the negative. Orange is a very energizing color, and can also attract immediate attention; however, too much of it can indicate foolishness or not being taken seriously enough.

- **Pink:**

femininity, love, tranquility in the positive, but weakness and inhibition in the negative. Pink can be soothing and attractive, but can be draining and overdone very easily. Avoid using it unless it clearly matches and represents your brand.

- **Brown:**

seriousness and warmth in the positive, but lacking in 'flavor' or taste in the negative. Strong browns can be helpful as accents, but a site completely done in brown can indicate boredom or lack of creativity.

Using powerful color combinations is very helpful when choosing the layout of your blog, and most blog platforms offer 'color combos' so you make the right choice. If you are designing your palette from scratch, just remember the principles of each color's psychological impact and proceed accordingly.

Columns

The number of columns in a blog has been debated time and time again, and there are both advantages and disadvantages of each. All blogs are set up in as one-column, two-column, or three-column structures. The best way to pick one is to simply choose something that suites your blog's purpose. For example, if you plan on linking out to partner sites or other blogs, you'll need a three-column structure. This will give you enough space to create a blogroll and relevant links on the right sidebar, include your blog commentary down the middle, and then put advertising and other links on the left side bar.

A two-column blog is most advantageous for a blog that has limited advertising. You will still have space for an extensive link roll and perhaps some contact information, but all reading will take place on the left side of the page.

A one-column blog is very basic, and is a good place to start if you want the blog to stand alone and *not* link out to different areas. This will help you create immediate interest to the content itself, and will definitely be less distracting for most web visitors and readers. Sometimes a minimal look works better, especially if you have a lot of content that requires attention.

Font Styles

Unless you are using a customized blog template, there are only a few standard font styles to choose from. This is not necessarily a bad thing, since most web users are becoming with the typical font styles such as Arial, Times New Roman, and Verdana. These are easy to read, and can help people 'scan' blogs much more easily. Choose a style that complements your website and company image, and you'll easily avoid using something that may not even download correctly on all web browsers. Just keep in mind the impact and readability of the text on screen, and you'll be making it much easier for all readers to continue reading.

Text Format

Blog posting works under a similar format as writing articles, and the more SEO-friendly you can make each entry, the higher the chances of reaching the top of the major search engines. When you are writing your headings and titles, be sure to include keywords as often as possible. Each title of your blog will become an extension of the URL, and this is what search engines can find and rank accordingly.

A well-formatted blog entry will also include bullet points and headings. Even though blog posts are generally much shorter than articles, developing a well-organized post will help increase readership and be more favorable to search engines. It's a simple step that many startup bloggers overlook, and can help significantly as you make your presence online.

Making sure that you tag and organize all blog entries is another important element of your blog site design and overall layout. Archives of each blog entry are automatically created for review, but you can organize each entry by adding 'Categories' and posting each item into the appropriate section. This makes it easy for people to find specific keyword-based posts, and will also help with search engine rankings.

Customized Blog Template Design

If you decide to do something a little more creative, you may want to pursue a customized blog template instead. Customized blog template services are offered by many web designers and companies, and give you the chance to pick exactly the colors you want from your own website's color palette. If you want to include a special font, logo, or other artwork of your own, this is your best choice.

If you have web design skills, try developing your own blog template with the basic layout elements in mind. A customized template can be made with the same elements of a typical blog, but you will have the freedom to place and organize it as you would like to. Alternatively, there are upgraded versions of blogger platforms available.

Benefits of Using a Free Template

Still, if you're new to blogging or simply can't decide how the color scheme and layout should come together, a free template will save you time and upfront investments. You can always change your color choices later, and can try different types as you go along. WordPress, TypePad, and Blogger make it very easy to switch between themes as you start publishing, but you'll want to settle on something well before you start marketing and promoting your blog. Changing themes and colors too often may lead to confused visitors, so be sure to make some final decisions before you move ahead with promotions.

A free template will be your best choice when you want to:
- Save time
- Start publishing immediately
- Cut down on initial startup costs
- Create a simple accompaniment to your website

Importance of Layout and Pageviews

The visible layout and overall look of your blog has a strong impact on steady web traffic, and there are many elements of basic web design to consider as you piece together the blog. Making sure that all the graphics, logos, headers, and fonts of your blog are consistent with your message will help you deliver information clearly. Avoid the temptation to fill your blog with random content and images; the quality of your postings is always important.

Making sure you are posting frequently is another easy way to increase page views. The more that people realize you are updating the blog regularly, the higher the chances of regular subscribers. You want to make sure your layout is attractive and can transmit the right message on every visit. This will create a unique experience, and help you develop steady readership over a period of just a few months.

Building Social Authority

Establishing credibility is both a short-term and long-term goal for your business blog, and more valuable information that you provide for your audience, the higher the chances of success.

Today's competitive blogosphere makes it challenging to meet the needs of your target market if you do not pay attention to quality and maintaining some consistent standards as you start posting.

People who are turned off by your blog are less likely to return; with thousands of blogs on similar subjects, it is easy to lose traffic because of a lack of experience, poor writing, or simply not updating your blog enough.

Valuable blogs receive ongoing traffic as they start showing up on directories and indexes across the web. These include sites such as:

- Technorati
- Daypop
- Blogdex
- Blogstreet
- Digg

All of these directories receive thousands, even millions, of visitors each day. Each item that is listed on the site receives ratings or reviews from other users, and you can start establishing credibility simply by joining. These sites also contain thousands of articles and topic matter related to your subject; they can serve as effective research tools when you are developing blog content, and can give you some valuable links to work with as you start developing fresh ideas.

When your overall site is indexed on these directories in the appropriate category, this also provides some credibility. People who are searching across these networks can see that your blog may be more worthy of attention, especially when you include a logo, title, or description for the catalog.

Important Blog Elements

There are some essential elements that your blog must have in order to be credible. These are a combination of the site structure and design, as well as the style and type of content you start posting. Each one is discussed in detail below, and the blog must include:

- Author name and company (if any)
- Contact information
- A brief Bio or About Us section
- Blogroll
- Links to resources
- Well-balanced visual elements
- A steady amount of ads
- No spam in comment boxes
- Compelling language and headlines
- Proper language, free from typos
- References to sources
- Carefully placed affiliate links (if any at all)
- Author responses on comments
- Appropriate language and conduct

You'll start with providing the author name and company; this is essential for helping your readers make a 'human' connection to your blog, and they should be able to contact you directly with any questions. Blog readers are looking for an 'insider' perspective on most issues, and it is very helpful for them to be able to distinguish company marketing materials from an actual first-person perspective. Knowing who the author is will help to bring the message of the blog closer to home.

This goes hand-in-hand with the contact information. You can include your e-mail address or even a phone number if necessary. The goal is to make sure users can trust that the information is coming from a real person, and they have the freedom to contact the author if necessary. This can help you create a connection with both customers and random visitors, providing credibility for your content.

Next it's a good idea to provide a brief bio. This can also take the form of an 'About Us' section that briefly summarizes who you are, why the blog exists, and what you plan to include. This can be helpful for anyone who simply stumbles across the blog and needs a quick summary of what your blog is about. This information may also be included on the homepage, as it can help direct users to the appropriate resources–your main website, for example— instead.

The blogroll is a very effective marketing tool, as it helps readers see who else is linking to your blog, and where to find more information. The blogroll is your connection to other blogs in the blogosphere, and credible blogs listed here will in turn help you earn some credibility. A blogroll should be comprised of at least ten to fifteen different blogs or websites.

It's a good idea to send out e-mails to everyone on the blogroll notifying them of the inclusion, and hopefully listing you on their blogroll as well. This will help boost traffic from other resources, while helping you link up to some valuable blogs for referencing as well.

The Resource Links section is another area that will demonstrate credibility; a solid resource list will inform your readers that you are using various resources for research and keeping up to date with news in your industry, and also provide them with other navigation options as they browse your site.

The resources links section can also be followed up with an e-mail to each website notifying them of the inclusion. They may choose to participate in a link exchange program as a result, furthering your chances of increased traffic.

It's important to remember that an attractive layout will help to boost your credibility naturally. The visual design and navigability of your site are important for your overall presentation, and making sure that there are no major errors in site design is an ongoing project.

The opportunity to include ads on your blog makes the site more valuable to advertisers, but it is important to remember balance during the selection and implementation of ads.

Overwhelming readers with ads, or simply bombarding random advertisements throughout your site can easily turn off a fair amount of first-time visitors. Even when you start joining affiliate programs and other networks, maintain a steady amount of ads that complement your site instead of distracting your readers from the content.

Monitoring spam comments is essential to keeping your blog in good standing, and will have a higher chance of reaching the top rankings of search engines when it is free of clutter and spam-related materials.

Spam blockers are often a part of most blog platforms, but even the filters can overlook some types of comment spam on occasion. Monitoring your blog regularly will ensure that you are keeping track of visitor comments, and you can select an option to moderate all comments before they are published if necessary.

This prevents spam bloggers 'sploggers' from overloading your site with unnecessary material without authorization, and can help you post the appropriate comments and feedback to keep your blog as interactive as possible.

Ensuring that your headlines are compelling, original, and creative will also help to reach out to your readers. Credible blogs make an extra effort to provide unique and engaging content, and your efforts will pay off when you are posting relevant information on a consistent basis.

In addition to the headlines, watch the quality of the content you are posting; use strong and effective language to deliver your message, and provide links and references to material as necessary. Editing your blog regularly is just as important as writing it and it should always be free of typos and grammatical errors.

Blog entries are designed to be short, concise, and compelling; avoid turning the blog into an article repository, and write blog posts that are only 300-500 words in length at max.

If you do want readers to read an article, direct them to your company website where they can view it in a different format, or provide a link to its home on the web. It's best to maintain consistency throughout your blog so that readers can become accustomed to your voice, tone, and style.

As you develop each piece of content, make sure you are providing references to sources. Even if you are redirecting users away from your blog homepage, you can use settings where the link opens in a new window. This will help them stay on your blog page if they need to, and providing the right references will help you establish credibility and authority on the subject naturally.

Watching how and where you place affiliate link ads is another element of credibility for your blog. If readers feel that you are simply using the blog as a vehicle for affiliate links, they are much less likely to believe that your content is coming from experience and not just a marketing ploy instead. We discussed the value of affiliate link programs in the previous chapter, and it is very important to keep this in mind as you start to introduce visitors to the blog.

Affiliate links are only valuable to your readers if you have found the products valuable yourself; if readers detect that there are ulterior motives to the placement of these links, they may simply stop visiting.

Keeping up with your blog also involves responding to comments in a timely manner, and appropriately managing negativity. Starting a 'flaming war' (Written online arguments with your contributors), will not help your reputation, and many startup bloggers make the mistake of losing focus when responding to comments on their blog. At best, it can be helpful to simply moderate comments before publishing so you can control the interactions on the site.

It is difficult to earn your reputation back after communicating publicly on sensitive issues, so be weary of this during your responses.

In addition to appropriate commenting, it's essential to use the right language and tone. Even though blogging is naturally conversational in style, it can be 'read' the wrong way without context.

Make sure you are using politically correct terms when necessary, and avoid writing posts that require reading between the lines. Offending large groups of people after writing seemingly simple posts can take its toll on readership; make sure to review and edit content as needed.

Search Engine Optimization

Search engines today are becoming even more refined and smarter at finding relevant and informative sites and blogs to index, and your blog will receive a higher credibility status when it encompasses most of the important elements. Search engines and directories are looking for:

- Relevant content
- Appropriate formatting and titles
- Steady visitor traffic
- Linking in from other sites
- Regular posting and updating
- Consistency in blog content
- Sites free of spam and excessive advertising
- Effective use of Ad Sense

Establishing Credibility

Making yourself a trustworthy and credible resource on the web takes time, but becoming an expert in your niche industry is an essential step towards regular readership. Even if your blog is an extension of your website, you can use it as a subsidiary resource platform that can help introduce readers to your company, and encourage them to continue reading. From the customer or visitor's perspective, there are essential signs of credibility that help distinguish one source form another. This includes:

- Longevity of the blog
  How long has it been active, how many posts are there?
- Experience
  Does the author have other sites and experience published around the web? If so, what are they? Expertise – can the author verify their expertise?
- Design
  Is the site well-constructed and updated according to industry standards?
- Writing style

Is the author a strong writer, or do they seem to post poorly written content on a regular basis?

- Readership

  Has the blog or site reached a high amount of readers? Many people turn to ranking indexes such as Alexa to determine this.

- Consistency

  Are the posts regular and arranged in the appropriate categories, or are they simply submitted to the blog randomly?

- Transparency

  Is the voice natural and friendly, or does it sound like it is coming from the marketing/PR department of the company?

Gaining steady readership will take time, but establishing credibility is a long-term goal for any blogger regardless of experience. Knowing how to convey a message that matches with your reader's interests is a necessary step; take the time to research, review, and edit your blog posts each time and make sure that the overall blog setup and design is in line with the competition.

Blog Traffic

Increasing Visitor Traffic, Promoting and Marketing Blogs

Tips for Increasing Traffic and Marketability

Earning blog credibility, increasing traffic, and promoting your blog in the process are all part of your marketing strategy. The only way you can build your brand is by becoming highly visible across a variety of domains; this includes blogging communities, social networking groups, and even discussion forums where your target market can be found on a regular basis.

Marketing and branding go hand-in-hand with your company website, and even more so if your blog is the only online entity of your business. There are a number of ways to develop a cohesive marketing strategy as you shift into the online world; this involves:

- Developing Relationships with other bloggers

- Identifying top blogging communities
- Determining a brand identity, and tracking its impact on your business

Build Relationships With Other Bloggers

No matter what type of visitor reaches your site—from the average guest to another blogger in your industry—there are many ways you can develop an ongoing relationship. Relationships are important in both the online and offline world, and a successful blog is often based on the first impression. Making sure you've taken the time to invest in site design and layout can help considerably with attracting a large audience. A blog can make a good first impression when it is:

- Easy to read
- Easy to navigate
- Provides useful and timely content
- Is built with categories and organized appropriately
- Offers archives filled with keyword content (easily indexed by search engines)
- Offers related posts
- Is consistent

Always remember that the blog represents your brand and is a virtual representation of your company. Communicating with your visitors and readers regularly involves your content, and understanding what they may be interested in reading will help you develop quality postings. When you are looking for fresh content to share, working with other bloggers will give you a chance to reach out beyond your scope of knowledge and make use of all of your resources.

Get Into Blogging Communities

Participating in blogging communities will ensure that you are deeply networked with other bloggers, and will help you increase your visibility as well. Blogging communities are rapidly growing across the web, but knowing which ones to join can be a challenge.

Some communities are simply not a valuable use of your time, and you can spend hours participating in discussions and comments with little or no traffic increases. A few blogging communities that can help you grow your business, however, do exist. You may try setting up profiles on:

- MyBlogLog
- Blogger
- WordPress Groups
- Google Groups

Blogger and WordPress both offer unique blog communities that you are automatically registered in once the blog is published. Since the social networks on these sites are so large, it can be difficult to make an impact immediately. The best strategy here is to use them as a resource for related blog content and identifying other niche subjects. Both of them are easily searchable and indexed and tagged by keyword categories.

Google Groups offers you an opportunity to create your own set of community users and 'fans.' Although this is generally casual in nature, you may find some value for your business based on a significant subject or topic.

Identifying a theme for your group is the first step; after registering, you will be able to recruit group members and can easily start promoting your blog and website links in an unobtrusive way.

Blog Ad Networks

Direct advertising is the most profitable way to advertise on your blog, but what's the easiest? Well, as you probably assumed form the chapter title, it's Blog Ad Networks. These networks pretty much do almost all of the work for you; all you really do is provide the blog. The reason we discussed direct advertising first is because it's quite a bit more profitable IF you have a very popular website.

If your website gets less than 1000 daily unique visitors then you might consider using a blog ad network instead. Blog ad networks will get you advertisers for whatever budget your blog permits. They will take a percentage of the profits; it's usually 50% but it can be less or even more. If your blog isn't popular enough to justify creating your own direct advertising campaign then having some revenue from ads is better than absolutely none. Using a blog ad network is also a great way to start out; once your website reaches a much higher popularity level or gains "authority" status then you can switch to direct advertising when you're ready.

Blog ad networks bring in vast numbers of advertisers who search for blogs who cater to their market. Bloggers get advertisers easier than most other sites because it is well known that regular blog readers are a bit more passionate about the blogs they read than regular sites, by and large. This is what advertisers are banking on, and in a big way.

My particular favorite ad network is called Performancing. One of the best things about it is that it's free to join. You get 70% of the ad revenue generated and they automatically adjust the price for advertising on your blog based upon page impressions (they track them with the code you put on your site). As your site grows in popularity, so does your revenue.

Getting advertisers for your blog isn't as hard as it used to be with blog ad networks doing the heavy lifting. Just make sure when you are checking out different blog ad networks that most of the money is coming to you and that your involvement in the process is minimal after getting set up.

If you are publishing in a decent niche, advertisers want what you have: a dedicated market! Take advantage of some of your blog real estate by adding revenue-generating ad space to your mix of profit streams.

Other Great Ad Networks

Here are some of the top Ad Networks that you can use for your blog:

1. **Google AdSense**

This one is a free program allowing you to display interrelated Google ads on your site. They offer competitive filter which enables you to filter competitors or advertisers; contextual filter, which eliminates delivery of ads found inappropriate for the page; editorial review, which means all Google ads are reviewed and approved before being provided on the page; and customizable default ads wherein in the unlikely event that Google is unable to provide your page a contextual ad, they allow you to place a default ad of your choice. Consequently, it doesn't just add up volume to your site but definitely lets you earn money. How? It is very simple. You earn just through valid clicks or impressions. It is definitely plain and simple. Just visit their site by clicking Google AdSense. Apply. Once your application is approved, you can get started in a jiffy. You basically copy and paste a block of HTML to your site and voila! Google ads will now start appearing on your site.

2. **AdOn Network**

This one now is a subsidiary of PV Media Group, Inc., which offers a full set of online media solutions from leading companies in online advertising, SEO, and more to form a first-class Internet marketing powerhouse. AdOn Network guarantees an innovative contextual and behavioral advertising solution to both advertisers and publishers to deliver quality traffic from the US and Global sources. It allows publishers, that is, you site owners and bloggers, to monetize your traffic from multiple forms of display and search advertising.

Their turnkey, private-level ASP (Active Server Pages) solution, AdOn Direct, allows you to create, manage, and distribute your own advertiser account. AdOn Network fully handle keyword management allowing you to concentrate on marketing and advertiser attainment.

Simply sign up. Then you can now get started. Create your own codes with just a few simple clicks and then you can now display contextual Banner Ads, Pop-Under Ads, Search Listing Ads, and Background Ads on your site.

3. Viral Ad Network

This one is used by, BBC, Nokia, Sony, Greenpeace, Polaroid, and easyJetsHotel. Yes, you read it right, coming straight from their site. All the world-renowned companies mentioned use this ad network on their site. Viral Ad Network offers a great deal of earning an income the easy way. It provides you with a high quality content the readers will surely love. This network is run by seven people at Rubber Republic, a specialist viral and buzz marketing company. They deliver a great deal of "addictive, ROI-driven creative campaigns and effective viral seeding services for clients like JVC, Easyjet, Warner Music and Sony," Viral Ad Network. Again, simply sign up and it would only take you a moment to start earning out of showing ads on your site.

4. Chitika

This ad network assures you to be a full-service, on-line, easy-to-use platform for receiving daily ad revenue. Chitika is made for both advertisers and publishers and it allows views only from the U.S. and Canada. You can use it with AdSense or as an AdSense alternative. Like any other search targeted advertising, they assure you to be able to display relevant ads on your site. And just like the previous ad networks mentioned, you simply apply as a publisher and then you can now get started displaying contextual ads on your site in just a matter of seconds. No hustle.

5. ValueClick Media

ValueClick Media is made for both advertisers and publishers and promises a leveraged "expertise, scale, extensive targeting capabilities and market leading optimization technology" to achieve both direct response and brand marketing goals. Publishers are further guaranteed that

ValueClick Media serves as a strategic buddy "offering a national sales force" and a complete suite of tools and services. This makes these publishers get the chance to earn the maximum possible income from a variety of online advertising inventory. Moreover, they offer you a great arrangement of quality advertisers, advanced technology, and superior support. As usual, it's easy to start earning through them. Simply sign up and them you can now get started.

Other reputable networks worth joining include Interclick, TribalFusion and Technorati Media. These are actually some of the top paying websites right now (giving you good rates and high percentages). Remember, using a blog ad network is the easier solution. After you've gained acclaim and popularity it's really a good idea to use direct advertising techniques unless you're just too busy to be bothered. You can greatly expand your profits when you're making 100% off of every click instead of 70% or 50%.

Make Use of Different Networks and Platforms

As you establish yourself across a variety of viewing channels and networks of blogs, it's still important to optimize your blog and ensure that all of your posts can be found easily. Submitting to sites such as Technorati, Digg, and StumbleUpon can help you earn respect from new readers, especially if you are providing quality information on a regular basis.

Increasing credibility takes time, but also requires developing a cohesive strategy across multiple online platforms and avenues. Some of the best ways to get found on the Internet are simply to join multiple networks, social networking communities, and publishing platforms. You can start by:

- Developing blog content that works
- Launching a Squidoo lens
- Promoting fresh content through article databases
- Increasing social networking presence, such as through Yahoo! Answers
- Link baiting on discussion forums and other blogs
- Introducing other authors on your blog or website, and coordinating a variety of PR tactics

Affiliate Marketing

Affiliate marketing is a marketing practice in which a business rewards one or more affiliates for each visitor or customer brought about by the affiliate's marketing efforts. This could include rewards sites, where users are rewarded with cash or gifts, for the completion of an offer, and the referral of others to the site. The industry has four core players: the merchant, the network, the publisher (the affiliate), and the customer.

The basic idea is that you provide special advertisements or links to a particular website and if the referred person buys from that website you get a commission on the final sale. This is usually between 10% and 50%. For example, you could provide a post about a particular online game that just came out and provide a link; when people sign up and pay for the game you get a percentage of that purchase for referring them.

Affiliate marketing overlaps with other Internet marketing methods to some degree, because affiliates often use regular advertising methods. Those methods include organic search engine optimization, paid search engine marketing, e-mail marketing, and in some sense, display advertising. On the other hand, affiliates sometimes use less orthodox techniques, such as publishing reviews of products or services offered by a partner.

The U.S. Federal Law on Advertising

Recent changes to federal laws prohibit certain practices while advertising to the United States. You should take note of this, especially when doing affiliate marketing. Here's the official statement:

"Federal law prohibits deceptive acts in or affecting commerce (15 United States Code Section 45). The Federal Trade Commission is charged with interpreting and enforcing that regulation. 2009 updates to the FTC's Guides Concerning the Use of Endorsements and Testimonials in Advertising (16 C.F.R. Part 255) make clear that the agency extends its application of the law to blogging and affiliate marketing.

Section 255.0 of the Guides defines an endorsement means "any advertising message . . . that consumers are likely to believe reflects the opinions, beliefs, findings, or experiences of a party other than the sponsoring advertiser, even if the views expressed by that party are identical to those of the sponsoring advertiser." A product review or blog discussion can constitute an endorsement."

What that basically means is that you should always disclose affiliate links and, specifically, avoid anything that could be construed as "deceiving." A good example would be a website that reviews the "Top 10 best web hosts" but in actuality just lists the web hosts by whoever pays the most for their affiliate link. This deceives users by making them think they're getting a genuine review when they're really just seeing the companies that offered higher affiliate commissions.

If you decide to use an affiliate program make sure that you disclose that you're making a percentage of the profit from those links. Many people will appreciate the honesty anyway.

More on the FTC

There's been a lot of furor over the "new rules" brought in December 1, 2009, by the FTC. Although, strictly speaking, these rules only apply to the U.S., if you do business with the U.S., it's a wise precaution to respect them. These new rules were meant to put an end to wild claims of 6-figure incomes in an impossible number of days, and curtail or monitor the practice of reviews that were actually 100% paid for, while masquerading as spontaneous, independent reviews.

It's your responsibility to have pages on your blog such as:

- Disclosure pages
- Disclaimers
- Privacy Policy
- Contact information or contact page
- Terms and Policies, if applicable

You can find the new FTC rules about endorsements on the FTC website.   You will particularly have to be on your guard about:

- How you disclose financial results from using the product you're reviewing – or even just telling your readers generally what to expect, income wise. You can no longer get away with "disclaimer" statements like "results will vary".
- Not disclosing your affiliate link straight away

You may want to download the FTC's new PDF, Guides Concerning the Use of Endorsements and Testimonials in Advertising.

What it boils down to, however, is that as long as you the correct disclaimers and disclosures, this should not affect you as much as some people would have you believe. Using a WordPress Privacy Policy plug in and generating your own policy at http://www.disclosurepolicy.org should do the trick.

But remember – seeking legal advice, checking out the new FTC rules for yourself and including the necessary disclosures is your responsibility.

Summary of Marketing Essentials for Promoting Your Blog

Now that you've covered the key elements of promoting, social networking, and joining blog communities, it may be helpful to reduce the concepts down for a summary. Here are the marketing essentials for promoting your blog; combining at least eight to nine of these as a basis for your first marketing effort will help you get ahead and start promoting your blog with much higher chances of success:

- Post high quality content on a regular basis
  If you are providing news on your site, average post amounts range from 3-5 posts per day. Make the most of your postings by only posting unique and high quality content. If you are looking to entertain or engage readers, aim for at least one posting per day.
- Enable automatic trackbacks and pinging
  Pings are a valuable way to notify search engines that your blog has been updated. Increase the chances of sharing blog content by enabling trackbacks on your blog.
- Make sure all posts are formatted and archived correctly

When you first start out, it can be helpful to leave this as a future project until you have developed some solid content. After that, take the time to sort through your content and make sure it is placed in the appropriate category. Also keep in mind that categories need to be based on keywords; you can gain a significant advantage with the search engines when you include high-ranking keywords on your category section.

- Develop your own link building campaign

Whether this involves contacting other bloggers, responding to comments and providing linkbacks, or simply making a 'call out' for links as you post, make sure you are keeping track of results and try a variety of strategies.

- Make sure your blog is optimized

Template optimization involves the URLS, RSS subscription buttons, and title tags are embedded appropriately. While most blogging platforms can help you do this automatically, you will need to pay attention to these areas on an ongoing basis.

- Submit any podcasts and media files to the appropriate directories

If you do start developing podcasts for your blog, make sure you are submitting them to the appropriate directories. Most are free, and can help you gain even higher rankings on the search engines.

- Comment on other blogs to develop expertise

Researching is just as important as writing for your blog, and you can search other blogs relevant to your industry and start commenting appropriately. Keep in mind the rules of the forum or group, and make sure your posts are relevant to the discussion. Always remember that your credibility is an important part of this, so be resourceful and post accordingly.

- Develop a glossary section

This is an often-overlooked opportunity for increasing search engine rankings, and can be a valuable resource section for your readers as well. A glossary can be as simple as keywords with definitions, and you can also start inter-linking the definitions to actual posts within your blog.

- Customize your blog and design it with your logo in mind

Even if you aren't launching with an exact replica of your website colors, choose something similar that will be attractive to your readers. Customized designs and templates are the best way to make a valuable first impression, but you may choose to wait until a later date.

- Setup a Google sitemap

Google sitemaps are designed to capture the key elements of your blog and validate them for search engines. This is one valuable step toward web optimization, and can significantly impact search engine rankings.

- Identify a list of authoritative blogs and other web sites

Even if you are not using these on your blogroll or link exchange program, knowing where to consult information can help you develop content on a regular basis. Create a comprehensive list of at least 15-20 sites that can help you post unique and relevant content.

- Make use of statistics

Statistics will help you track results and easily see fluctuations in visitor traffic. Most blog platforms are equipped with statistical analysis programs, and you can watch trends and patterns daily.

- Promote yourself on social networking platforms

These are essential for gaining exposure and a strong presence alongside your target market, and you can join different groups and communities very easily. Setting up the right profile will take some strategy (see Chapter 7), but is an important element of building your social community presence.

- Submit links to social bookmarking sites

This is a very effective way to promote individual pieces of content. As soon as you have created a URL of your submission, that link can be promoted across multiple channels and networks in just a few steps. Try submitting to the major social bookmarking sites such as Technorati, Digg, and StumbleUpon for increased exposure on highly valuable topics and content. Even interacting on these networks can help you learn what types of content and topics your audience may be looking for.

- Position yourself as an authority

Consult valuable resources and give appropriate credit on your blog. This is not only helpful for your readers, but can help you establish yourself as an expert within your field.

- Focus on building credibility

  You can build credibility by communicating directly with other bloggers in the industry; establish a guest blogging opportunity for other bloggers to participate, and encourage them to market their contributions in the process.

- Make contact with bloggers offline as well

  You can still build credibility and enjoy networking in the offline world, and attract some new visitors the 'traditional' way.

Advertising Your Blog

Monetize Through Advertising

Direct Advertising

One of the ways to monetize your blog is by accepting blog advertising from other advertisers, such as text-based or banner advertising. Specifically the most profitable way to do this is by directly selling your advertising space instead of using a third-party company to network your ads. Direct advertising is arguably the best method to monetize a website. Here are some of the key benefits:

Benefits

- **Bigger Profits:** The main advantage of selling your own ads is the fact that you will cut the third party out. This will increase your revenue potential. For example, let's say you sell text link ads on your sidebar through a certain company, and the text links sell for $80 monthly. Since you are using the company network to sell the ads they get maybe 50% of that price, and you will end up earning only $40 a month for each text link. Regardless of what you actually got to keep, someone was still willing to pay $80 for a text link on your blog. So why in the world should you share that with someone else?
- **Freedom:** It's true that large advertising networks have access to a wider pool of advertisers and they have more credibility to close the deals. That being said, if you have all the requirements in place and spend some time looking at the right places, you should easily be able to sell your own ads just as efficiently as the larger networks.
- **Adaptability:** Another great advantage of selling direct advertising is that you will have much more control over where and how the ads will be displayed (i.e., you can avoid intrusive advertising). Google AdSense is nice but, unless you blend it with the content, it's annoying some of the readers and you will get terribly low click-through rates.
- **Credibility:** Lastly, having sponsors and direct advertisers on your blog might help your credibility. Even small and poorly done blogs can stick some AdSense units here and there. Having established companies that are willing to partnership with your site, in contrast, can show users that your content has quality and that the site is somewhat professional.

Before you jump into selling your own ads you should be aware of some of the potential hazards and problems you could face:

Potential Problems

- Time: Selling your own ads has many advantages; however, it's not a cure-all. The biggest drawback of this advertising option is the time that it will consume. This time will be spent optimizing your website for the ads, finding potential advertisers, negotiating with them, and handling the administrative matters (e.g. making payments, tracking statistics, delivering reports etc.).
- A Lot of Rules: Selling direct adverting is not as easy as making money from Google AdSense. You will need to have a popular blog, a professional looking design, special software etc.
- Volatile Market: Unless you close deals for very long periods (which is unlikely) you will find yourself looking for new advertisers or optimizing your website to attract new ones every other month. The opposite is true for most advertising networks; for these you just need to plug some code and they will do the rest of the work (If your site or blog is just a hobby, therefore, direct advertising might not be the best option).

If you've decided that direct advertising is for you then the very first thing you have to do is actually find advertisers who want to advertise with you. Before you start trying to get advertisers you should go over your blog and make sure it's really focused for this purpose. I've read many articles that said the general rule of thumb is 2000-4000 daily visitors before incorporating advertisements into your blog. That's actually quite a high number but you should definitely have an established customer base before you try to get advertisers. Here are some broad guidelines for what you should already have in place before you start your advertiser search.

Before You Start

- **Be Popular**: Before landing direct advertising deals you will need to have a good amount of traffic on your site. I don't necessarily agree with that 2-4000 rule I mentioned earlier; but generally, I recommend around 1000 daily unique visitors. If you are below that mark you should focus on building traffic instead of looking for advertisers (Or use a third party company until you gain enough traffic). Other factors like Google PageRank, RSS subscribers and Alexa rank might also help.

- **Know What You Want**: You might have one of the most popular sites on the Internet but unless your site also has a very clear niche and a defined audience, advertisers will not find it very attractive. We discussed this earlier in Effective Blog Writing but for those of you who may have skipped that section, I cannot stress this enough! You should avoid rambling about 100 different topics on the website; advertisers want to deliver a message to specific people, and the more specific the better (usually).

- **Look Professional**: If you are planning to monetize your blog through sponsors you really should invest some money into a professional looking design. Advertisers will be associating their product or service with your blog and not too many of them would be willing to get mixed with an ugly or amateur-looking site. If you know all about web design that's great but maybe, just for this project, hire someone with a degree and a guarantee.

- **Required Software**: In order to serve your ads, rotate banners and track statistics you will need to install an Adserver. If you are looking for a simple solution you should try WP-Ads. This WordPress plug-in will serve ads for specific ad zones that you create. The only drawback is that it does not count clicks (only impressions). If you need a more sophisticated solution check OpenAds. You will need to spend some time learning how to use it, but it offers virtually all the features you will ever need.

- **Clearly Define Ad Space**: It is very important to have an *"Advertise Here"* page.

- On this page you want to give some details about the website, like audience, traffic and any other factor that might be of the interest of potential advertisers. Don't just leave empty, blank spaces in places where you'll be accepting advertising. State clearly that those spaces are for sale. Create an image that says "Your Ad Here" or "Ad Space for Sale" and place your image in the exact spot where the ad will appear.

- It's also important that those spaces are clickable links. Then you make those links point to a page that clearly tells advertisers who they can get the space to advertise in. This means you'll need to create a specific page that is solely for listing all the prices, terms and conditions for different advertising spaces. Don't forget to add a contact form or an email address that allow people to contact you directly. Not all templates and themes will be suitable for selling direct advertising. Preferably you want to have an idea of what kind of advertising you will sell (468×60 banners, 125×125 banners, text links etc.) and design your website according to those objectives. Advertisers want visibility so reserve a good spot for them and cater to your specific advertisers.

- **Payment Options**: You might have everything in place, but if you are not able to cash payments – or more importantly, if advertisers are not able to pay easily – you will end up losing deals. PayPal is the best option here. Notice, however, that a personal account will not suffice. You will need at least a premier account to be able to accept credit cards.

Pursue Your Advertisers

You don't have to just sit around and wait for the offers to come in. In fact that's probably a terrible idea; you can just as easily go after advertisers yourself. By seeking out advertisers instead of just waiting for them you can choose and accept advertisers that you like instead of just dealing with whoever shows up. When you're e-mailing advertisers to see if they want to advertise on your blog, don't forget to provide the following information:

- Introduce yourself briefly.
- Explain why you are e-mailing them.
- Tell them why you could really use their advertising.
- Explain the benefits and features of advertising on your blog.
- Include details on your price, terms and other information on advertising on your blog
- Tell them about what the theme of your blog is and how it related to what they might advertise there (and how it will land them clicks).

A great way to go about this is to create a standardized letter that you use for all advertisers with their contact information changed. Just follow the previous guidelines and make sure the letter is easily editable so you can keep a template and modify it for each different advertisers. After that information the advertisers should be able to decide if they are interested or not. If they reply, then you will fix the details. All of that information should be contained in 2 or 3 paragraphs. If you send a mini-novel to potential advertisers they will just skip it altogether. Remember what I said way back in Chapter 1? People have low attention spans!

Where to Look

Once you have your direct advertising program established, you will start to receive inquiries from people. In the beginning, however, you will need to hunt advertisers down. Do not get discouraged if get turned down initially, provided you have all the aforementioned requirements, sooner or later you will find someone willing to take a shot on your site.

- **Link-Backs**: If a company is willing to link to your articles or to add your website under its "Links" or "Resources" section, it is also probably willing to discuss about advertising on your site. You need to keep track of those incoming links. Link-backs are possibly the most important aspect of advertising your own blog. Google page rank and, more importantly, Google results are almost entirely based on links back to your site. If your site has a ton of link-backs then your potential advertisers will have a ton of clicks and your blog will be especially favorable (it all goes back to being "Popular").

- **Comments & E-Mails**: The same principle applies to people leaving comments on your blog or sending you e-mails. If you see an employee or the owner of a company among them that could be interested on your website then contact him or her and get the conversation going. You may have just found a potential advertiser!

- **AdWords Users**: Throughout your search for advertisers you will notice that most of the established companies are not aware of the benefits of online advertising. If a certain company is already spending money on Google AdWords, it is very likely that they would also be open to other forms of online advertising. Think about some keywords that are related to your topic and do a Google search for them. Check the sponsored links that will appear and contact them. (You can also check the advertisers that appear on the AdSense units of related websites.) An even more advanced tactic would be to use Google's AdWords Keyword tool to find a host of related terms to look up.

- **Other Ad Networks**: While Google AdWords is, by far, the largest advertising network there is, there are many others that could be useful. Check the companies that are spending money on AdBrite, Text-Link-Ads, BlogAds, SponsoredReviews, DoubleClick and similar companies.

- **Banner Ads on Similar Blogs**: Check out popular blogs and websites on your niche and see what companies are advertising there. This is a great tactic that we'll discuss in detail in the next section; the gist is that you can find out what they're advertising and offer them a better or comparable deal.

- **Bookmark Potential Sponsors**: Have a bookmark folder on your Internet browser and label it "Sponsors" or something similar. Every time you come across a company or site that could be interested in sponsoring your blog, bookmark it. It's always good to stay organized and this will allow you to queue up a list of potential sponsors that you can tackle whenever you have some free time.

Sponsorship and Research

Blog sponsorships are continuously becoming a trend online. It is because an increasing number of businesses have noticed the power of blog as an extension of their marketing campaign. Under blog sponsorship, you are going to work closely with your advertiser and actively promote their product and service in your blog post. Moreover, your blog will also carry advertiser's brand name and company logo.

By the way, you can close a sponsorship deal by separating a section on your blog that is solely for promoting your sponsored product. Such kind of blog advertising works very well if your blog is already very popular and has a lot of visitors who comes to your site regularly.
Another way to find blog advertising opportunities is by using keyword research. Keyword research is not only for affiliate marketing but also it can be used in finding blog advertisers. Here is the process:

- Start by doing a search based on the main keyword you are currently targeting in your blog.
- See if there are any ads that are currently posted under this keyword, if yes; find out those companies based on the web site URL.
- Contact them and see if they are interested in advertising on your blog.

Exchange Links

Other blogs that exchange links with you before may be also a potential advertiser. It is because if they find your blog and exchange links with you, chances are that they find your blog that is full of potential so that they want to exchange link with you. Therefore, you can send them an email and ask if they are interested in posting ads to your blog.

The Power of Branding

How Branding Can Help Your Business Prosper

What Branding Can Do For Your Business

Take a look around your house at some of the products you purchase on a regular basis. Why do you choose a particular brand of maple syrup or toilet bowl cleaner? Chances are you recognized the name on the label or the logo and on the packaging and were "presold" because you connected that name or logo with quality. You may not have even read past the name to make the decision to purchase.

That's the power of branding. When you can connect your product or service with a reputation of quality and trust, you catapult yourself into household-name status. It doesn't matter whether your business targets only a small geographical area or if you market on an international level, the power of branding can be immense. Blogging can help this effort along greatly, but it is not the only thing you need to consider. There are several other components that must go into a successful branding effort to make it pay off.

Ingredients for Successful Branding

Blogging and other marketing efforts can build up the hype behind a brand and really get people talking about products and services, but more is needed to make this kind of effort pay off. To establish the kind of trust that is required to create a positive reaction in clients or customers, the products or services behind your line must also offer:

Quality – Branding builds recognition for a product, but that product must still have the quality needed to impress customers. You simply cannot gain positive brand recognition unless your products and services offer the kind of quality needed to elicit trust in your customers.

Excellent service – Customer service is everything in business and has been for a long time. When building a brand, customer service can boost word-of-mouth advertising. This, in turn, boosts referrals and helps a brand grow even more. Even in businesses where no product or service is sold directly, such as blogging for a living, customer service still matters. People will trust the authority of a blog if posts are written with authority and integrity. These things can also be built upon with timely and well thought out responses to comments from readers.

Value – This is a big buzz word with customers these days. If your product or service comes at a price, make sure buyers get the value they are after. Value doesn't mean "cheap;" it means quality for the price point. Even free blogs that host advertising can have "value." In this case, the information shared needs to be accurate, informative or entertaining. In short, readers need to feel like they haven't wasted their time by visiting.

Branding simply builds on all the key ingredients in a successful business and puts them in a package customers can readily identify. When you offer solid service, high quality and value, your products will begin to speak for themselves. New products or services will be more likely to have instant footing in the market simply because of the brand. In short, branding enables you to build on previous successes to grow your customer base and launch new offerings more effectively.

Brand Development through Contests and Giveaways

There is no denying the fact that people love freebies. This is especially so online. If you want to generate a lot of interest in your blog and the brand you are trying to develop, running periodic contests and offering giveaways can be incredibly useful. Contests can include chances to win the products or services you are branding. Giveaways might include "starter" products or even free eBooks and other tools readers might be interested in.

- The benefits of using giveaways and contests to promote your brand and your blog include:
- The buzz they generate.
- The chance to gain new visitors (customers) who might not have otherwise taken the time to look at your blog or even your brand.
- The free advertising that can be created – other Web sites and blogs will often write about contests and giveaways that might be of interest to their own readers.
- The chance to develop loyalty among visitors who take the time to check out your products or services.

When your intent is to build a brand through a blog or any other means, advertising is important. Consider some of the bigger brands out there and pay attention to how much they actually put into advertising. Even companies that have reached the "household name" status still put a lot of time, energy and money into advertising well after they've been established. This is to help ensure that that their brand name remains in the forefront of customers' minds and that new customers are constantly gained.

While you might have budgetary constraints, do try to use a multipronged approach for advertising. The more places you can get your brand name advertised, the better. If money is a concern, focus on cultivating free advertising options such as basic SEO, word of mouth and incoming links. Should money not be an issue, a combination of free and paid advertising techniques can help build brand recognition and ultimately help you succeed in your efforts.

Blogging Is Just a Piece of the Puzzle

While blogging is a highly viable and important piece of the branding puzzle, it is not the only component that should go into an overall campaign. Beyond the written support found in a blog, a solid effort to create a brand presence may also include such things as:

- The use of an identifiable logo to create a visible brand.
- The use of the brand logo in any/all advertising efforts, including print and television.
- The use of the brand name in sponsorships and contests to generate a buzz and a sense of good will toward customers.
- The use of a brand logo on letter head, business cards and other written materials.
- When the desire is present to build a strong branding campaign, the use of brand identifiers should be widespread. The more the company, product or service logo is seen by the public, the better.

Branding can help take a good product and the company that puts it out and turn it into a household name. The creation of a well-designed blog can boost efforts greatly and give a company an avenue for getting the brand name out to the public on a regular basis. When this format is used to its full advantage, it can help catapult a brand while developing a rapport with readers.

Developing Content

Tips for Developing Effective Blog Content

Making Your Blog Work

Making changes on the type and style of posts that you submit can also be helpful; take a look at sites such as Lifehacker and even the Digg blog itself for some ideas on how to present a variety of posts and styles. Images are important, and linking out to videos or other examples across the web can also improve the quality of your submission. Working with different writing styles and presenting information in a new way are just as valuable to readers as a simple article, and can increase readership easily over time.

There are a number of ways to write good, effective blogs. Not all of them involve you actually sitting in front of a computer and writing blog posts every day. There are a ton of blogging services that can actually do it for you if you choose. Personally, I recommend creating a template and doing it yourself, but you can choose whichever strategy best fits you. The key points here are brevity, information type, target-audience and quality of content.

Brevity

Brevity, or briefness, is something that many commercial blog posters take for granted. Somewhere in their quest for the perfect keyword ratio and inserting the right amount of product links they fail to realize they're writing mini-novels instead of regular old blog posts. The average blog post is between 150 and 500 words. Anything below 150 can probably be considered a micro-blog and anything over 500 is really pushing your readers.

This depends, of course, entirely on the subject matter of the blog. If you have a science blog and you're discussing quantum physics or string theory then you might legitimately have 1,500-word blog posts. Those types of intellectual discussions require a certain amount of explaining and it's hard to write fluff for them. If your blog is about fashion trends, however, it's unlikely that you'll want to have extremely long posts.

Visuals

People in general do not have extremely large attention spans, especially when they're browsing content online. If your blog is visually a large block of text, many people will subconsciously find it insurmountable and avoid it because they don't want to read it. This is why it's good to keep your blog posts as short as you can. If you have a subject matter that requires a long post then you can increase the likelihood of it being read by visually splitting up the blog post.

You could separate it into two different posts for part 1 and part 2. If you separate it in just the right place you can make each blog post stand on its own and people will be intrigued to read the rest instead of afraid to try and read it all at once. Another thing you can do is adjust the spacing of your post. Use paragraphs and do a hard return after each one. If you have key points, use bullets. Try to keep your paragraphs at no more than 3-5 lines and avoid anything that looks like a large, rectangular block of text.

Blog Topic

Keeping your blog on topic is extremely important, especially when we factor in search-engine optimization. If your blog is all about editing videos then you should expand on that topic but don't wonder off too far. Related subjects might be: video editing software, editing techniques, effects training courses, cinematography books and colleges that offer video-related degrees. Try to find between 3 and 5 related topics within your blog's niche and stick to them. If you constantly write about a certain subject and have a lot of link backs and proper keywords, you become a lot more likely to be considered an "expert" by the search engines. If your video editing site becomes popular you could have prime spots in search engines for terms like "video editing" or "special effects." This is also known as becoming an "Authority" on a subject.

The main benefit of exploiting your niche, aside from search results, is to become appealing to advertisers within that niche. If your website has first-page results on Google or Yahoo for video editing results then you will be extremely desirable to any company who wants to advertise video-editing products or services. Your value goes way up within your niche and you can charge even more for advertising. You will also get a lot more affiliate purchases for products that have to do with a niche you are an authority of. People are more likely to buy a product if it's endorsed by a popular website that is considered an authority on the subject.

You may not have to "nichefy" your content if you have an extremely popular blog. You still need to keep your blog within a slightly-focuses section but you can make it broader. For example, you could have a blog about visual art and in that blog you could discuss video editing, special effects, painting, drawing and 3D art. Your possibilities are greatly expanded but you still retain a major theme that all of your posts and updates will follow. This reduces your chances of becoming an authority on any particular subject but it increased the variety of advertisers you have to choose from.

Sometimes having many different advertisers can be better than having many from a single niche. For instance, if DVD sales are in a slump and your blog is about buying DVD's then you will have much less advertisers. If your blog was about buying all types of Media then you could pick up the slack with advertisers from different companies like MP3 Distributors or Blu-Ray

Player Manufacturers. What you sacrifice in niche-sales you make up in stability. A multifaceted blog is harder to start up and harder to get daily clicks but the added stability gives you better growth potential and more longevity.

Target Audience

This all plays into the target audience. Who exactly are you writing for? Knowing your target audience is absolutely essential if you want to get anything done with your blog. Some key points include: Their field of interest, their age, their gender and their educational background.

Audience Interest

The first thing you have to consider is what your target audience is interested in. Your blog could be about DVD's in the general sense but what readers are you targeting? Are you targeting people who want to buy DVD's, people who want to make DVD's or people who want to read DVD reviews? You can choose all three if you like and your blog can just be about everything DVD-related but you will probably get more return visits if you focus on one subcategory within your main topic.

It's also a good idea to pick two or three topics that go especially well together. For example, your blog could focus on reviewing computer parts and where to buy the parts for cheap. This is a perfect combination because people who are buying computer parts generally want to see a review before they buy (Likewise people seeking reviews are generally seeking to buy). In this way you've taken your target audience's top two priorities and catered to them. What you want to avoid is posting off-topic with things that might fit into the broader category but don't actually make sense within the context of your blog. If you're targeting people who want to see reviews for and purchase computer parts then you really shouldn't have a random post about a new PC game. This fits within the broad category of computers but it's unrelated to your actual blog.

That's not to say you can't make off-topic posts; they just need to tie into your theme. Using our previous example, you might want to make a random post about a recall on a recently released computer part or a post about the exact computer set up that a celebrity or other person of interest is using. It's good to introduce newsworthy items that relate to your blog but aren't necessarily on-topic because they bring diversity to your pages.

Target Audience Age Group

It's never a good idea to discriminate or alienate a particular audience but that doesn't mean you can't target a specific audience and optimize your blog for them. If your blog's topic is dealing with menopause then your target audience is probably going to be women who are between 35 and 50 because they are the primary types of people who are affected by menopause.

Bearing this in mind, you don't want to use a lot of Internet lingo that's popular with teenagers today. Your readers are not going to take you seriously if you sound like one of their children or grandchildren. Instead you should keep a mature tone and write with a slightly informal and empathetic voice. You can research other blogs that cater to your age range and see how writers focus their content to a particular group.

Teens and young-adults between 16 and 24 are generally people who grew up in an age where the personal computer was commonplace and relatively inexpensive. They understand Internet slang and popular themes that get passed around on social networking websites. Adults ages 25-40 are generally more mature (if only slightly) and may or may not be familiar with Internet slang etc. This age group will have a higher income and many people in this age group will have families. Adults ages 41-60 quite often have families and will not be impressed by Internet slang or sites that aren't family-friendly. Of course these are rather broad outlines; your blog's niche market may be senior citizens who ride around in baker gangs—anything's possible. You can do more extensive research on demographics and how to use them to your advantage for the best results.

All About Gender

In terms of marketing for a specific market: Sometimes. Generally the nuances that you'll adjust for gender differences are pretty subtle. There are a few instances where it makes all the difference. If you're website is about buying the right prom dress then your target audience is obviously women (specifically teenage girls) only. That's not to say women are the only people buying prom dresses but that is where the majority of your clicks and affiliate purchases will come from and that's who you are targeting with your blog. Unless your blog is related to a gender-specific product then you can pretty much decide for yourself if you want to market for a specific gender.

Sometimes it makes sense to market for a particular gender. Video games, for example, are classically geared towards males in the 12-24 age group. This has been an industry standard for years since research shows the most sales from that group. That being said, you might be alienating a whole market of potential readers and customers. In recent years the video game industry has found that they've lost millions in sales due to advertising campaigns that were considered to be misogynistic. If you think that targeting a specific gender will increase sales then go ahead but the general rule of thumb is to try and create a blog that both genders can enjoy.

Education

Here's one that a lot of people overlook when they're thinking about their target audience. A blog is primarily just textual articles that people read so it's essential that you don't confuse your readers with content they understand or offend them with content that's too simplified. So what is the educational background of your target audience?

Well, if your blog is about construction then think about the requirements of the job: for entry-level positions and even most management positions you only need a GED or high school diploma. For some management positions a person might need a degree in business or architecture. From here we decide who our blog appeals to: Upper management or entry-level and general worker positions?

The purpose for this is to assess what knowledge they already possess. If you're targeting experienced construction workers then you need to either avoid talking directly about the semantics of construction or carefully check all of your facts; you don't want them to notice any misinformation and stop taking your blog seriously.

The other point of this is to deliver content that your audience will understand. Obviously if your blog is about tips for getting your GED then you're not going to want to write it with the prowess of a college English professor. Conversely, if your blog is about becoming a teacher then you certainly don't want to over-simplify it or have any type of grammatical mistakes. People won't take your blog seriously if they feel it's "below" them and they won't continue reading your blog if they can't understand it. You need to establish the educational level and background of your target audience and try to cater to it.

When in doubt, take a conversational tone and type as though you normally speak. Make sure you don't have any grammatical mistakes and avoid using slang words and colloquialisms (a word that only has meaning in a particular region). As I just did, you can define certain words in parenthesis if you think they're words that aren't common or are often mistaken for other words.

Controlling the Quality

The quality of your blog content is one of the most crucial aspects of having a successful blog that draws in potential customers and clicks to make you money. If your blog is filled with inane or unorganized posts you won't be able to maintain a user base. If your blog is filled with automated posts that don't feel human you won't get indexed by search engines and if your blog is just of an overall poor quality you're not even going to get visitors. How you handle the quality of your blog depends on how much time you personally have to devote to it.

The best way to control the content of your blog is to write it yourself. Nothing matches the freedom and control you have when your content is being generated by none other than you and if something goes wrong you only have yourself to blame. This is also the cheapest method of running your blog. If you're reading this book I can only assume you want your blog to make money for you and the best way to do that is to cut your costs as much as possible.

Once your blog does become popular you might find that it's actually beneficial and time-effective to hire someone to update your blog for you. This will probably be something that you freelance out to people on a weekly basis; it's not exactly something worth creating a part-time job for (and the costs of that would be astronomical). A good way to do this is to use a micro-project service like Amazon's Mechanical Turk service. This allows you to give out micro-projects where you pay a freelancer a small fee to write a single blog post. If you're keeping with my advice on brevity then you should usually only need posts that are under 500 words so you should be able to get those created for under $10 a piece which is an absolute steal. If the subject matter or post permits it you could separate a single blog post into 3 or 4 different 50-75 word micro-projects and pay as little as 50¢ a piece! Then you can pay another person a few cents to piece them together or do it yourself.

As nice as that option is, you have to determine if your blog really requires it. If the time it takes you to post the jobs on a freelancing website, describe them and then approve or deny them is going to take longer than just writing the blog yourself you might want to skip those services.

All About Grammar

The most basic, rudimentary thing to remember about writing your blogs is that you need to have proper grammar and spelling. You don't have to go crazy with figurative language or use unnecessary advanced techniques but there's nothing less impressing than having a simple spelling mistake in a blog; this is especially damaging when you're writing about something intellectual like biology, architecture or grammar! Here are some common mistakes that you can be sure to check for before every post:

Word Confusion

This one is particularly annoying for me. People often confused words that are similar or words that are homophones. Homophones are words that sound the same but are spelled differently and mean different things. Here's a brief list of commonly mistaken words and how they *should* be used:

There: "I'm going over there today. "

They're: "They're my best friends ever!"

Their: "I borrowed their car last Sunday."

Your: "I like your shirt."

You're: "You're a nice person."

Whose: "Whose shirt is this?"

Who's: "Who's that knocking on my door?"

Its: "Don't touch its spikes!"

It's: "It's very hot in here."

Affect: "That doesn't affect me." (Verb)

Effect: "What are the side effects?" (Noun)

Than: "Oranges are better than apples."

Then: "I saw a movie and then I went to the store."

Loose: "This belt is loose, my pants may fall down!"

Lose: "I didn't want to lose the game but I had fun."

Whole: "I have a whole candy bar all to myself!"

Hole: "There's a hole in my favorite shirt!"

There are many others, but those are the most common mistakes that people make all the time. These types of mistakes seem minor but they really can have a detrimental effect on your return traffic. Another problem is when you use words that or just incorrect or simply don't exist. Here are a few prime examples:

- *Copywrite:* There's no such thing. A Copywriter is a person who writes copy; copyrights are the rights to a work.
- *Irregardless:* Again, this doesn't exist. There is only the word regardless.
- *Ironic:* Ironic usually means something that is unexpected or the opposite of what you would expect. Use of this word to mean "comically unfortunate" is ubiquitous so this is a fairly harmless mistake.
- *Deceptively:* While this is technically a word it has very little legitimate context. People will generally know what you mean but try to find a better alternative. (e.g. instead of "The water was deceptively shallow" you can say "The water was much deeper than it looked.")
- *Alot:* This is incorrect. A and lot are two different words; this should say instead, "a lot."

General Quality Issues

Now that you've prepared yourself for writing quality blogs without embarrassing grammatical mistakes you should look over the general quality of the content. Are you using images in your blog? Make sure they're not too compressed and look good on your blog. Pick relevant images that are of decent quality. Make sure not to load your blog up with too many images or some users might experience slow load times and just avoid your blog altogether.

Keep a schedule of when you're going to update your blog and try to stick to it. If your blog develops a lot of regular readers they probably know your update schedule and visit your blog accordingly. Make sure your blog has an RSS feed and find the URL that you can use to advertise your RSS feed on other websites. Every blog software is different so you'll have to do some extra research on yours and find out how to set up your RSS update feed.

Promotion and Publicity

As you establish yourself across a variety of viewing channels and networks of blogs, it's still important to optimize your blog and ensure that all of your posts can be found easily. Submitting to sites such as Technorati, Digg, and StumbleUpon can help you earn respect from new readers, especially if you are providing quality information on a regular basis.

Increasing credibility takes time, but also requires developing a cohesive strategy across multiple online platforms and avenues. Some of the best ways to get found on the Internet are simply to join multiple networks, social networking communities, and publishing platforms. You can start by:

- Developing blog content that works.
- Launching a Squidoo lens.
- Promoting fresh content through article databases.
- Increasing social networking presence, such as through Yahoo! Answers.
- Link baiting on discussion forums and other blogs.
- Introducing other authors on your blog or website, and coordinating a variety of PR tactics.

Blog Post Elements

Here is a checklist of all the elements that go into a great review blog post:

Blog Post Checklist	
Intriguing headline that makes the reader curious. *Use only one long-tailed keyword phrase per blog post. Don't "keyword stuff".*	If it feels natural to do so, put your keyword for that post in the headline
Introduction	- If it feels natural to do so, repeat your keyword phrase within the first paragraph - Let the reader know which product you are going to review

Image	- **Use only photos that are:**
	  A. Original, and owned by you
	  B. Have a public domain or Creative Commons license
	  C. Royalty Free
	And check the licensing terms – even within Creative Commons licenses, terms can differ greatly. That being said, **screenshots of your product** in action and **promotional graphics provided by your product seller** work the best, especially for purposes of Review Blogging.

Pros and Cons	
How it Works (if applicable)	
Proof	
Conclusion	
Call to Action	
Include your Keyword!	(Don't forget this point!)

Let's go over these one by one, in a little more depth…

Your Post Headline

This is one of the most important aspects of creating strong review posts. Think back to all the most intriguing posts you've read. Why did they catch your attention?

- *Ask a Question* – In many cases, you'll find they asked a question. Instead of just "Jean Solar Powered Fountains" as your post heading, change it to something along the lines of "How Long Do Jean Solar Powered Fountains Really Last?"
- *Number it* – People like things they can quantify. "3 Things No One Ever Mentions About Jean Solar Powered Fountains" is far more likely to intrigue curiosity, too.
- *Diss it* – What are people really looking for, when they search for reviews on the net? They're looking to see if anyone has gotten scammed by the product creators. So play along with it – honestly, of course. If there's one feature you didn't like or that didn't work for you, don't be afraid to let people know about it: Doing that will set you far apart from other reviewers who only gush. Human nature being what it is, "The Single Biggest Drawback of using Jean Solar Powered Fountains" will catch people's attention quicker than "The Single Biggest Advantage…"
-
- *Be Controversial* – don't do this just for the sake of doing it or being obnoxious, but if there's something relevant to your product review that goes against popular practices, don't be afraid to hint at that in your headline (but make sure you follow through). For example, "The One Time You Shouldn't Use Jean Solar Powered Fountains".

Your Introduction

A good introduction should have a strong "hook" to make the reader want to keep reading. You want a show stopper of a sentence – but don't forget, show stoppers aren't always the most sensational sentence. They are, however, sometimes the most unexpected.

Relate the introduction to your reader. One way is to use "you" words. "Where were you, when Internet marketing began online?" But however you start your post, quickly introduce your product – "Search tools have come a long way since the 1990's, and Handy Dandy Niche Tool is about as far from its roots as you could get."

Most of all, however, your introduction needs to quickly summarize for the reader which product you're going to review, what it does, and who makes it. Do this – and then make doubly sure you cover each one of these promises.

Putting Images in your Posts

The latest data suggests strongly that images enhance a blog's readability and attractiveness – but there are some small but important "do's" and "don'ts" you'll want to keep in mind.

Don't make the image huge, and do make it relevant.

In a product review, usually your image would be a screen shot or a graphic provided by the product merchant: However, if you can come up with another relevant image – especially one that's unexpected or unusual (but still really appropriate even to the dimmest of readers) – go for it.

If you can't create visual interest with an image, then do it instead with white space. Break up your text with subheads and bullets. Make it visually easy to scan for information – Internet users are turned off by dense chunks of text.

But the most important image to use on your review blog?

Yours.

Seriously, people will come to identify you with the good information they're reading.

Get a gravatar, if you haven't got one already (those images of people you see in blog comments, linked to one of their email addresses).

And make sure your name is on the post, if you've got yourself logged in as "admin". You can do this either by including a by line, or a resource box for yourself at the beginning or end of the post. (It does improve "branding" of your persona as an authority figure. Otherwise, people often forget who is writing what they're reading!

TIP: If you use a professional theme such as DIY Themes' famous <u>Thesis</u> theme for WordPress, you can include **bylines** and **signatures** really easily.

Pros and Cons

Of course, you want to include the pros – but don't be afraid to tackle the "cons", too. To find out what sort of problems people are worried about, with similar products, try to figure out extra terms they might be searching with in Google, and work from that.

A word of warning, however… It's true people will input the word "scam" beside any product they're not sure about, when searching in Google, like so…

But if a product <u>isn't actually scamming someone</u>, resist the temptation to make that word part of your post, just for SEO purposes. If you ignore this suggestion and go for the easy catch, and your reader clicks on your link, and sees instead of an honest scam report, glowing praises of your product, with the careless disclaimer, "Jean solar powered fountains are no scam", you will rapidly and completely lose all credibility in her eyes.

Some other words that people use in searches that you may be able to substitute for "scam"…

- Review
- Flaw
- Drawback
- Problem
- Not worth it
- Rip-Off

Use Wordtracker's free keyword tool and try out your own potential search terms, relating them closely to how you, yourself, feel about your niche tool product. Feel that it's got a flaw? Look to see if there are any searches in the free keyword tool for "niche tool flaw". Feel that it's more of a glitch? Try searching with "niche tool glitch". The best way to figure out what your niche customer would search for is to literally put yourself in his place!

A final word about reporting flaws in a product – always remember <u>flaws can actually be seen as an advantage</u>, to some people.

Example: "It's true that the Handy Dandy Niche Tool is ridiculously easy to use – but this is offset by the fact that it's not highly customizable for those who need a more in-depth statistical analysis. It is definitely the "for dummies" version of a niche finding tool – only simpler!"

Now, if your entire target market is composed of complete newbies, this "flaw" is likely to appeal to them greatly! You weren't being dishonest – but you were **positioning** your flaw to actually become a benefit.

Of course, if your review blog was called "Advanced Marketing Techniques", this wouldn't work at all – its simplistic, foolproof operating mode really would be a disadvantage – but if you're running a blog called "Marketing for Newbies", you're home free.

How it Works

Most products benefit from a brief description of how it works.

This doesn't mean you have to spill all its creator's secrets. It does mean you should focus in on one aspect you're particularly pleased about, or hit what you consider are a number of high points. ("The first benefit that sets Handy Dandy Niche Tool apart from its competitors is…")

What you are doing is drawing a vivid mental sketch for your reader of the reasons this tool will work for him or her. You really don't need to provide a step-by-step manual, and take all the mystery out of it.

Proof

Anything you can do to provide proof of the benefits you're revealing will go a long way to solidify the impact of your review on your reader. Be very careful, however, about income claims – the new FTC rules are very specific. If you mention how much money you made using a system, not only have you got to be able to prove it with actual documentation, you also need to provide an overview of what the average user can expect – and that representation has to be provable too.

But there are other ways to provide "proof" too. You can do things like:

- Quote the number of sales since its release
- Show screen shots of some wonderful benefit (e.g., a great keyword phrase turning up in your Handy Dandy Niche Tool)
- Quote the complete lack of refunds (providing your figure is accurate)

Conclusion

This is just a short paragraph wrapping up the other end of your "parcel", and mirroring or echoing your opening statement: For example, tying back to our fictional opening statement: "Where were you when Internet marketing started online?", we might conclude with something like: "You may not have been even aware of the Internet when marketing online started, but sales aids with advantages of Handy Dandy Niche Tool can certainly help you get ahead of the pack now."

Your Call to Action

But you're not quite done yet. Now comes the most important part of your post – your "Call to Action".

As marketers, we're all familiar with this principle – yet it's surprising how many people actually fail to include it!

What is a call to action? In the particular case of review blogs, it's simply making sure your reader knows how to instantly access the product, if he wants to purchase it – in other words, you provide a link. And don't forget to tell him, even though it may feel like stating the obvious, to go visit it.

If you've written a "non-review" post – something just to provide your readers with really valuable information about their niche – you can finish with a different type of call to action: One which positively invites comments.

This concluding statement can be as simple as:

- "Comments, anyone?"

- "Like what you've just read? For more reviews as they happen, subscribe to my RSS feed below."
- "For more information on [your review's topic], check out [affiliatelinkname.com]."

No matter what you're posting about – even if it isn't a review – always include that call to action. (If nothing else, it's 50% more likely to generate comments – and comments are good!)

More on SEO and Keywording

Using SEO and Keywords to Optimize Your Site.

Understanding SEO

Search Engine Optimization, or SEO, involves manipulating the content on a Web site to work search engines like Google and Yahoo to your advantage. When people use search engines, they type in keywords and keyword phrases. These queries result in the search engines delivering a listing of sites that best fit the terms the users typed in. Ideally, you want your blog to show up high on that list when terms related to your niche are punched in by potential readers.

To make this happen, your blog will need to target specific keywords and phrases related to your niche. You'll want to use these words and phrases frequently, but logically, within your content, on metatags, photos and more. You won't want to go overboard and "stuff" keywords into content, but you will want to make the best use of words and phrases that are related to your niche.

Selecting the Right Words

Choosing keywords to build a blog around isn't as difficult as it sounds. Search engines like Google even have programs that can help you select words and phrases that are commonly used by searchers to find information and products related to your niche. If you'd like a lower tech way to go, you can even sit down with a pad and pen and just brainstorm words that fit in with what you do and who you are trying to reach.

To target your use of keywords on your blog, consider such things as:

- What you do – If your blog will be dedicated to selling a particular product, you'll want to rank high for the brand name, of course. You'll also want terms related to it. If you sell baby blankets, for example, consider words related to your products that go beyond the brand name. "Custom baby blankets," "crib linens," "baby bedding" and so on might be terms worked into your content on a regular basis.
- Geographical cues – Sometimes it can pay to use geographical cues within SEO efforts. If you're a doctor in New York, for example, chances are you want to pull in highly targeted readers. While you might not mind visitors from California, your business would benefit more from visitors from your home state or city. With this in mind, temper your keywords with geographical cues when possible. If you are a dentist in Queens, you might want to attract readers who are looking for "Queens dental offices" or "Queens dental experts." If this is the case, use these terms in your post to boost your rankings.
- When picking terms for SEO purposes, it is often best to have a fairly decent sized list to work with. If it's your plan to update your blog daily, working only with "custom baby blankets" can become highly repetitive too quickly. Just create a well defined list and work the chosen words into content as much as possible without losing the clarity of your posts.

Why SEO Matters

Taking the time to work a SEO plan into your blogging content is an extra step you probably didn't count on. It can, however, greatly boost your branding efforts and help launch your site off on the path to success. There are a number of reasons why it pays to consider SEO in your overall branding and blog marketing plan. They include:

- The potential traffic – Search engines do provide an outlet for free advertising. When you manage to rank high for your selected search terms, you'll gain traffic, which can increase your branding success and even your sales.

- The targeted nature of the traffic – When people visit your site, you want them to be interested in what you have to offer. It doesn't matter whether it's a product, service or just information. If your visitors arrive from searches related to your niche, they will be more likely to be interested in what you have to sell or say.

- The pre-sell factor – If a visitor finds your blog because he typed in "toothbrushes for sale" and that's your business, that visitor is already in a buying frame of mind. This can translate to a near instant sale if your products suit his needs.

- Linking – When you rank high with the search engines, your blog can gain increased publicity from other sites on the Internet. The more credibility and ranking you gain, the more likely it is other sites will quote yours and refer to it. This can help you increase your branding efforts and enable you to gain even more free recognition for what you are attempting to do.

More on Keywords

We've spoken about using a strong keyword for each post. While this is a good, solid guideline, it's not a hard and fast rule. Sometimes you'll come across a keyword that has almost no commercial value, yet in your tiny sub-niche, it's the "buzz" topic of the moment.

How do you find these "buzz" topics? More crucially, how do you become the first one to clue on to these "buzz" topics?

One suggestion is to take full advantage of Google Alerts. If you have a Google account, with a gmail address, you can set Google to notify you – immediately, daily or weekly – whenever your keyword phrase, name, subject or web URL is mentioned. Many top marketers use this as an invaluable aid to "predicting" the next topic.

Using social media such as Twitter, Facebook, Digg, Stumbleupon, et cetera, is also a proven way to see where people's attention is turning in real time. You can also monitor hash tags and keywords via platforms like Twitter, using RSS searches.

Finally, instead of relying on free keyword tools alone to find profitable niches and products to mine, you can invest in paid products. Some of these carry a hefty price tag, but are stuffed with all the bells and whistles you can imagine – and more.

Content Pitfalls to Watch Out For

Maintaining a blog can take some effort and it is easy to fall into some traps that can hurt your search engine rankings and even your brand image. Some of the potential pitfalls to watch out for include:

- Keyword stuffing – Keywords and phrases are very important for gaining recognition from the search engines. They do not, however, trump the need for quality in your content. Use keywords where they naturally fit into content, but don't force them.

- Posting for the sake of doing so – Remember, you are trying to build up a brand image. This means you want to truly appeal to visitors. The best way to do this is to offer content that will be of interest. Don't just put anything out there in hopes you'll pull in traffic. Take the time to consider unique and interesting posts. It's better to skip a few days if you must than to just post for the sake of doing so.

- Duplicating content – Refrain from posting the same thing over and over again. Duplicate pages will be spotted by frequent visitors and they can hurt you in regard to search engine rankings.

- "Borrowing" content – While it is acceptable to quote other sources in your content, don't just borrow it without giving credit where it is due. When you quote another site and give credit this creates a link to the original site, which is important. We'll discuss the reasons for this shortly.

Once you have put together a rough plan for your posts, the search engine terms you'll use and your message, you'll need to start populating your blog with content. The maintenance of a blog can make or break its effectiveness in helping with overall branding efforts.

Using Tags for Optimization

Learning how to optimize each of your entries is essential for search engine rankings and gaining visibility. In order to make sure your blog posts are finding their way to the right communities and categories, it's a good idea to take the time to learn how to tag each post appropriately.

Tagging is relatively new to the Internet, and has gained more prominence with the onset of Web 2.0 applications. More and more websites are using tagging as a way to sort and aggregate data found across the web; not only is it visually appealing when it appears on larger aggregator and search engine sites, but it gives people easy access to find relevant information much faster and in a more practical way.

Learning how to use tagging to your advantage can help you develop quality blog posts and a share-able set of content. Tagging systems are also known as 'folksonomies' as they are created by people all over the web; although you will be creating the first set of tags on your own to categorize your data, don't be surprised to come across your post elsewhere on the web that has been tagged with even more keywords. These are simply ways for people to find and search different portals more easily. You can stay one step ahead by using resourceful and easily identifiable keywords.

Categories vs. Tags: Knowing the Difference

Both categories and tags are ways for you to organize your blog entries, but there is a noticeable difference between the two. Categories make use of a 'tree' to organize data, blocking off particular categories into subcategories and identifying content accordingly. They are highly structured, similar to indexing books on a bookshelf.

Tagging offers a different opportunity; instead of organizing content in a linear manner, everything is organized by association with a brainstorm-like effect. It is a very non-linear way of organizing information, but strings together keywords so you are in essence, 'breaking apart' each submission and identifying it with a simple word.

Many bloggers forego tagging because they think readers can simply search and find the information using the search box. This is true in some cases, but some posts may not be so easily accessible. Tagging helps both the readers *and* the search engines. SEO-friendly blog posts and articles can gain easier recognition when you tag entries appropriately, and also provide users with a simple way to track down information in a few clicks.

Types of Tagging

There are two main types of tagging for blogs: internal and external.

Internal tags are those that are used exclusively within a site. In these cases, you may have set up your own tag cloud, or are creating a database of highly-searched tags for easy reference.

An external tagging system makes use of social bookmarking sites such as Technorati, or del.ici.ous where each submission is picked up by these larger aggregator sites. This helps with dispersing your content much more easily, and you can broaden the reach for a particular piece of content by participating in these external sites as well.

Learning From Tag Clouds

A good place to start when developing tags is to look at tag clouds on your favorite community portals and search engines. High-traffic websites use these clouds as ways to interlink information found throughout the website; this generates an assortment of keywords that are similar or relevant to your topic matter, and can help you gain an understanding of what is popular (or not) at any given time.

The Built-In Search Box

If your website has a built-in search box, tagging will also help users retrieve relevant articles and posts immediately. Using tags with search functions is a great way to provide visitors to your site with easy access to all your articles, posts, and related materials. Not only that, these same tags are posted to larger sites such as Technorati and Digg automatically.

How Do I Implement Tagging In My Blog?

There are various ways to implement a tagging system on your blog, and most blog platforms support the standard tag plug-ins to get started. A few leading plug-ins and options include:

- Ultimate Tag Warrior
- Jerome's Keywords
- TechnoratiTags
- SimpleTags
- Yahoo! Keyword Tags

- **Ultimate Tag Warrior** helps to provide both internal and external tags, especially those that fit right into Technorati, Wikipedia, and social bookmarking sites such as del.ici.ous. The tags are displayed after just a few clicks and can make the tagging process much easier.

- **Jerome's Keywords** is another tool that displays a list of tags and then makes it easy to simply implement your selection. This tool is ideal for WordPress blogs, and can easily help you find the right topics and keywords with a few tweaks.
- **TechnoartiTags** are ideal for Moveable Type platforms, and use a similar feed as Ultimate Tag Warrior to send to larger aggregators such as Technorati.
- **Yahoo! Keyword Tags** is actually a generator that you can place right into a WordPress blog as a plug-in. This will list a set of suggested tags and keywords, making it much easier to simply copy and paste, or type the list of tags directly into your tag box. This works hand-in-hand with Technorati and will help you avoid the need to go in and brainstorm tags for each post or subject.

Tagging and Marketing: Effective Market Research

When you are browsing and exploring other blogs and sites of interest, reviewing tag clouds for keywords is a great place to start. Tag clouds give you the benefit of literally 'seeing' which keywords are of prominence; this means that more people are reading and writing about that specific item, and you can develop your content and blog posts accordingly.

Regular market or industry research is essential to developing quality content for your blog. Not only will you be able to create content that is highly-readable, but you'll also have a chance to appear next to other relevant, and often leading blogs, in the industry. No matter what type of business blog you are developing, you'll have a chance to reach out to your target market in a more effective and approachable way when they can track down your information after just a few clicks.

Blog Maintenance

Maintaining Your Blog

Taking Care of Your Blog

Now that you have a blog, you have to come up with a plan to keep it maintained. When you're trying to build a blog up to boost branding efforts, the maintenance of the blog will matter a great deal. To pull in traffic and turn a casual visitor into a customer or a frequent visitor, you'll need to offer things they want to see, read about or can actually use.

Maintaining a blog does take some work, but it can be a rather fun process. The more useful and frequent entries are, the more likely it is you will be able to develop a following and a rapport with visitors.

While there is no set formula for how often a blog needs to be updated, frequency can prove to be important for gaining rankings and traffic.

Options for Maintaining Your Blog

While many people choose to build and maintain their own blogs, this is not the only option available for you. Keep in mind that "content" doesn't always have to mean a written post either. Images and videos can also serve well here and assist in keeping a blog looking fresh. Some of the avenues you can take to ensure your blog is updated on a regular basis include:

- **Using inside writers** – You can write your own posts or have people within your company contribute. Depending on the size of your company, you can spread the responsibilities to different staff members that might be able to help with content that will assist in building up the brand. For a corporate brand, for example, the marketing department might write the majority of posts. Their posts, however, can be complemented with articles written by product developers, the CEO, engineers and so on.

- **Hiring professionals** – Depending on the niche topic your blog will focus on it is possible professional writers can be hired to add updates. These writers might post about their own experiences with the niche or your product. They might also keep the blog fresh with interesting industry related news and events. Professional companies and solo freelancers can add a new perspective to a blog that helps to build branding efforts while making posts more varied and interesting.
- **Using guest writers** – It is also possible to ask other niche-related industry professionals to write posts for a blog. Guest posts are an excellent way to vary content and keep it fresh and interesting. This technique works very well for certain products, news blogs and other similar pursuits.

Think Multimedia

Blog content does typically center on the written word, but visuals can also make a huge impact. To make sure your blog supports your branding efforts and is also appealing, be sure to include a variety of different presentations.

Some of the options here include:

- **Photographs** – It's not a bad idea to include an image with every post or nearly every post. If you're writing about how your baby blankets are hand-knitted, show an image of one being created. If your blog focuses on horror movie news, be sure to include publicity shots that relate to a particular film you are discussing. Photographic images can support your content and pull readers in for a closer look.
- **Videos** – Creating videos to support posts or to be used in place of a standard post is also a great way to go. Videos might explain how to use products, show how they are

made, demonstrate related accessories and so on. If you're blogging to create a branded news site, consider using footage related to your posts.

- **Audio** – Podcasts and other audio pieces can vary the content on a site and make it more appealing to visitors.

-

It is not necessary to use multimedia presentations for every post or even very often. Occasional use, however, can really add value to your content. These additions can also be used on their own in place of posts, which will help you create a more fluid site. Remember, readers are more likely to return frequently if they A.) like what they see, and B.) know content will be fresh and new when they visit again.

Frequency of Posts Matters

Imagine picking up a newspaper and reading the exact same stories that appeared yesterday. You wouldn't be happy. Chances are you'd never buy that newspaper again. The same idea holds true – almost – for blogs. Readers like to see new content on a regular basis. This gives them something to look forward to and it can also help with your branding efforts.

There is no particular rule on how often a blog should be updated. If you are working on gaining credibility for your blog and your brand, more is often better. It is frequently recommended that updates go into a blog between three to five times weekly. It is also best to make sure the updates are spread throughout the course of several days each week.

When posts are updated frequently, your branding efforts will benefit because:

- *Frequent posting can help with increasing the keyword density on your blog*
- *Your search engine rankings can go up*
- *You give visitors more reasons to return*
- *You provide more points of entry into your blog so people can learn about your brand*
- *You give yourself more of an ability to establish your blog as an authority on the subject matter*
- *You increase your chances of having content that others will want to quote and link to, which can increase your traffic*

Launching your blog and putting some content on it is not enough to really help with branding efforts. To get the greatest benefit from the project, you do need to pay attention to updates and make sure your content is relevant to the topic, useful or enjoyable to readers and fresh.

While you can build traffic on your blog through SEO techniques alone, it does make sense to also employ some forms of advertising. This is especially so if you are trying to build a brand name. When you first start out people will not know to turn to your blog for information unless you tell them to. This is where a supporting marketing plan can really benefit your efforts.

Final Words

Some Important Reminders Before You Start Blogging

In Conclusion

No matter what type of business you are in, building a brand name does take some effort and dedication. A blog can serve as a very useful tool for helping to build recognition for a brand and to promote a greater sense of loyalty among customers.

When a blog is created specifically to boost brand name recognition for a product or service – or even if the blog is the brand being promoted – you will want to put some thought into the launching and maintenance of this vehicle. A well-maintained blog can help you increase interest in your brand while also raising its credibility level.

To get the most out of your blog, remember to:

- **Create a functional, attractive format** – You want your blog to be easy and enjoyable to read. If visitors have a hard time reading the text or navigating the site, they may not return.

- **Send a clear message** – Select guidelines for your entries and pick a base style to follow. This will help readers know what to expect when they make return visits.
- **Give visitors value** – Make sure your entries relate to your branding niche and offer readers something of value such as useful information, entertainment or even news they might be interested in.
- **Keep the site updated** – Blogs are meant to be consistently updated. Try to make sure your site is fluid and offers visitors plenty of reasons to refer it to their friends and to keep coming back for more personally.
- **Think visual** – Make sure to mix up your blog with text and images both. This adds impact to your blog and does appeal to visitors.
- **Get the word out** – Branding is a process that requires a lot of positive attention to pay off. Advertising in one form or another can be extremely important for the traffic numbers on your blog and the overall chances of success for your branding effort.

Remember to re-invest some of your ad income into your own advertising ventures so you can increase the traffic to your website. The more traffic you get the more income you'll get and the more you can advertise; it could become "Viral" rather quickly if you play your cards right. Follow the guidelines and stay on track and in no time you'll be able to turn your regular old blog into a veritable virtual goldmine!

Blogging is an effective and excellent way to get the word out about a brand. When this format is used to its greatest potential, you can reach out and literally tell people and show them why your brand is worth trusting. In turn, thanks to the two-way communication offered in the blog format, your followers can also add to your brand's credibility and help boost its reputation even more through their own contributions.

Presented by Robert & Toby Maggard

http://Sleepy-Dragon.com